The Lownsbury Chronicles

Lownsbury's Lecture

Featuring

The Bowtie Principle

and

The Syndromes of Civilization

Lownsbury's Lecture is offered as a compendium to The Lownsbury Chronicles. Featuring the philosophy and ideas of Professor Larimer Lownsbury, amid an entertaining and fast moving lecture. Lownsbury's Lecture is an enjoyable and stimulating look at the birth and death of civilizations. It offers an insightful look at mankind's modern day placement inside of his own history, and various phenomenon that perpetually surround his existence.

Presented as a non-fictional, philosophical narrative set amidst an inspired contemporary environment, Lownsbury's Lecture offers a unique look into the mind of the most provocative character of W.C. Wallbaum's exhilarating time travel series; The Lownsbury Chronicles.

The Lownsbury Chronicles:

By W.C. Wallbaum

The Machine; First Strike

Lownsbury's Lecture; A Compendium
Featuring
The Bowtie Principle
and
The Syndromes of Civilization

Coming Soon: The Machine; Second Option

The Lownsbury Chronicles

Lownsbury's Lecture

W.C. Wallbaum

All rights reserved.

First Edition Copyright: 2018 by W.C. Wallbaum

Cover art and illustrations by: Cat's Imaging and Design

The Bowtie Principle and The Syndromes of Civilization and related graphics are the exclusive creation and copyright of

Wall To Wall Publishing

Walltowallpublishing.com

ISBN: 978-1-7331256-1-1

Acknowledgements

Special thanks goes out to all the American patriots that endeavor to awaken their civilization and educate their children.

A well deserved appreciation also goes to Pixabay.Com.

Lownsbury's Lecture

Featuring

The Bowtie Principle

and

The Syndromes of Civilization

W.C. Wallbaum

Bowtie Principle

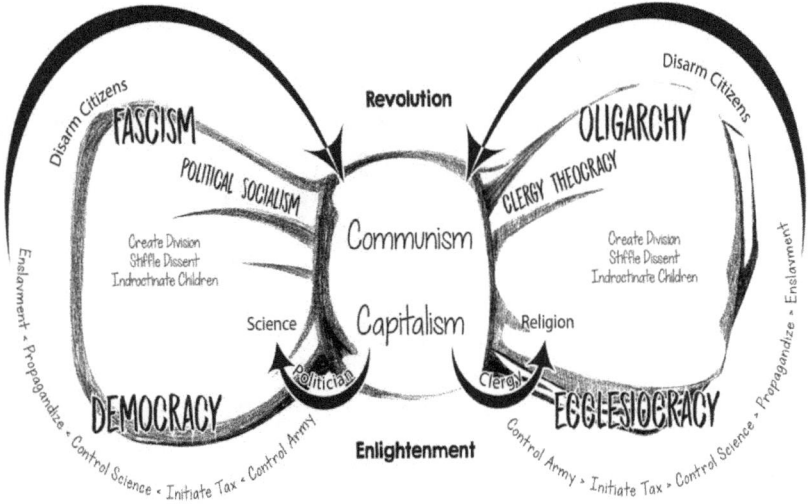

Revolution

Disarm Citizens

FASCISM

POLITICAL SOCIALISM

Create Division
Stiffle Dissent
Indroctinate Children

Communism

Capitalism

Science

DEMOCRACY

Politician

Enlightenment

Enslavment ◦ Propagandize ◦ Control Science ◦ Initiate Tax ◦ Control Army

Disarm Citizens

OLIGARCHY

CLERGY THEOCRACY

Create Division
Stiffle Dissent
Indroctinate Children

Religion

ECCLESIOCRACY

Clergy

Control Army ◦ Initiate Tax ◦ Control Science ◦ Propagandize ◦ Enslavment

Forward

Dear Readers,

I remain secluded in a remote cabin, working tirelessly on compiling the notes that had been given to me by Professor Lownsbury for the second installment of the ongoing adventures through time with Jack Sterling, Larimer Lownsbury, and Will Masters. But, I have taken a small respite to introduce, what I believe to be, an equally intriguing set of documents. A lecture I had intended to publish long ago, but was side tracked at Professor Lownsbury's request.

When I released *The Machine; First Strike*, it included a forward in which I briefly described my first encounter with Professor Larimer Lownsbury. An encounter that deserves further description and elaboration.

This has also become an observation that has been shared by a number of you.

Responding to requests concerning my initial meeting with Doctor Larimer Lownsbury, I have chosen to publish the lecture in which I had first become acquainted with the man. A lecture that I had personally found intriguing, and one which led me down a path of enlightenment known to so few, yet sought by so many.

I present for your consideration, this historical and philosophical compendium to *The Machine; First Strike*

W.C. Wallbaum

"Regulation is the government sanctioned tyranny of the minority."

--Professor Larimer Lownsbury.

∞

"When somebody tells you that you are thinking too much, it will usually mean that they are not thinking enough."

--Deb Wallbaum

∞

"He alone who owns the youth, owns the future."

--Adolph Hitler

∞

"The farther back you can look, the farther forward you are likely to see."

--Winston Churchill

ONE

Introduction

Of all the names bandied around the water cooler of the paper mill in which I was employed, none were spoken of with more malicious antipathy and downright venomous hatred than that of Doctor Larimer Lownsbury.

His name had been spat with disgust by most of my more passionate colleagues. (More so even than against the degenerates that frequented the tabloid pages.) And barely given a complimentary nod by the more reserved among them.

As a greenhorn, syndicated columnist, I naturally became intrigued as to who this man was and why he created such a vitriolic hatred among my peers.

"A history professor? Really?" I would ask.

But, it was widely believed among many of my colleagues that Professor Lownsbury was a quack. That he knew nothing of what he spoke. That he was a racist, a homophobe, a xenophobe. (And, the typical list of biting cliché's would be spewed *ad nauseum*.)

Even by this time, however, I had grown increasingly wise to this transparent and disparaging stratagem. Understanding the trite aspersions as attempts by the pedestrian of my profession to stifle dissent, and causing me to question their actual ability to create a thoughtful viewpoint of their own.

What I found very curious though, was that although most of my colleagues spoke with certainty of Doctor Lownsbury's inner most thoughts, none of them were able to convince me that they even had a basic knowledge of the man's work. I couldn't find a single colleague who had ever even heard the professor speak. And, if I asked these same opinionated critics if they would agree to attend any of Doctor Lownsbury's lectures, each would resoundingly answer, *"No."*

I began to realize that the castigation of the Professor by these so called, *'intellectual'* peers of mine, was rooted in a determination to remain ignorant, and a mindless willingness to simply espouse hateful propaganda.

I eventually succeeded in gaining audience with a handful of people that *had* attended Doctor Lownsbury's lectures and found most of them had been very impressed with the man; his ideas and philosophies. Some were not entirely convinced of their accuracy, but each spoke with a high level of respect for his ubiquitous charisma and knowledge. And, each one sharing the same advice; insisting that I should go hear for myself.

I didn't know what to expect as I entered the lecture hall of our local state college. But, I wasn't quite prepared for the acrimony of a handful of protestors that lined the sidewalks outside of the lecture hall. Their signs against *Fascism* and chants of *"Safe Space"* seemed inconsistent with the viewpoints of those I had interviewed who had attended Doctor Lownsbury's lectures. But, they seemed wholly in line with the pernicious viewpoints of my fellow journalists.

It seemed evident that these protestors existed within the same *group think* as that my colleagues; ignorant and acrimonious. I came to a glaring conclusion that these young people had never listened to Doctor Lownsbury. Instead, like my contemporaries, they had merely been indoctrinated with some kind of disinformation and were acting purely on a misguided belief.

As I watched these protestors, my mind teetered with a distinct, yet vague awareness. An epiphany perhaps, lingering just outside of my conscious reach. As if some great awakening remained just beyond my grasp.

I suddenly became more intrigued by Professor Lownsbury's imminent lecture; certain that a promise of revelation existed just inside those lecture hall doors.

The endorphin fueled feeling began to slowly fade from my consciousness as I realized a program had been shoved into my hands. Operating solely on auto-pilot, I took the offered pamphlet.

It was the proverbial agenda given out at most events. A small booklet of papers designed to correspond with the lecture that was about to take place. But, I paid scant attention to the items inside as I struggled to maintain my tenuous hold on the rapidly fading predilection. The understanding that the literature would be deciphered in due course.

The lecture hall was packed with a comingling of people from every walk of life. Some had found their seats and were waiting patiently, while others converged upon a nearby snack table. The murmuring of the group was a perpetually increasing cacophony of indistinct sound, like swarms of cicadae buzzing through the tree tops. It was a bit disorienting given the euphoric wake in which I remained.

A short man in a uniform jacket was making his way through the throng, shaking hands and giving directions for some purpose or another. I could see him directing several people to seats near the front and concluded that he must be an usher.

On the dais, I noticed that there was a large white board, divided into three sections, and each section covered with a corresponding drape of cloth. The contents beneath waiting to be revealed.

Another small white board stood on its own to stage left of the larger board. I could see that this lone display board was mounted upon a wheeled easel that could easily be manipulated.

Other items on the dais included a grouping of chairs, both to stage right and to stage left. A single chair occupied center stage. The groupings of these chairs appeared purposeful.

There was no podium, but instead a small table occupied the center of the dais, upon which a shiny, receptionist, press button bell was seen to be resting. Only a microphone stand and microphone awaited near the grouping of chairs stage right.

I took my seat and dove into my inner thoughts as I am prone to do, still beleaguered as to why, and how, a philosophical history lecture could be such a contentious subject to so many people. Even more disturbing was the militant response of those that had never bothered to sit through the class.

As I was pondering these questions, and trying in vain to grasp the epiphany whose elusive shadow remained just outside my reach, a finely attired figure emerged from the crowd and walked to the microphone. Removing the device from its stand, the man flipped the switch and the speakers came to life.

He introduced himself as the dean of the school as he expertly brought the crowd to attention and steered the stragglers to their seats. The murmuring of the rabble slowly descended until a warming silence surrounded the hall.

The preamble was short and perfectly enunciated, "It is my great pleasure to introduce a man who needs little introduction," the dean began. "Professor of history at the New England University of Connecticut, Doctor Larimer Lownsbury."

Applause resounded through the lecture hall as a tall, lanky man approached the center, his hand extended good naturedly to the dean. His skin was a light cocoa complexion and his close-cropped, curly hair was graying in perfect unison to the stubbly beard he sported. He wore a suit coat that was neither shabby, nor flashy.

Although his dress reflected the stereo-typical persona of his vocation, the rumored energy that his presence projected had been an understatement. There was indeed a wisdom that radiated from him with an almost visible aura. His eyes were like a window into an unfathomable intellectual power. I felt as if his gaze came to rest purposefully on me as he scanned the crowd before him.

I was rudely shaken from my awe though, as several young people jumped up from various points in the crowd and began screaming. I had a hard time deciphering what they were yelling, but it eventually became clear. The steady chant of *"Safe Space"* echoed through the hall.

It was more of the non-sensible slogans I had heard outside the lecture hall. It seemed laughable, since the mere act of screaming the words would seem to indicate that they were already in a safe space. I had a hard time figuring out what their goal was and what they were protesting. Nothing but an introduction had been made, and Professor Lownsbury had not yet opened his mouth to speak.

Again, that elusive epiphany danced along the outer reaches of my conscious. Daring me to grasp it. I was certain that the answers to the enormous questions of why these kids were so animated against ideas they had never heard was a key ingredient of this realization. But, the feeling remained fugacious. As if it were a blood curdling scream trapped within the hollow silence of a vacuous bubble; vestigial and unsatisfying.

I could see Professor Lownsbury tilt his head to the side, listening intently to what these youngsters were saying. As if they were entangled within a deep intellectual dialogue.

Members of audience began to shout back bits and pieces of rationalized arguments to these young people. Each attempting to reach them with logical bits of reason. But, then quickly giving in to the futility and falling silent with a shake of their head as another audience member would take up the attempt.

Eventually, as the audiences' anger began to swell in tandem with that of the protestors, Professor Lownsbury looked at his watch and lifted his eyes to a guard, offering a subtle nod.

Immediately taking their cue, several guards began gently pushing and guiding the protesters to, and through the doorway, and into the outer hallway. Locking the doors behind them and taking positions to prevent re-entry.

Lownsbury remained silent for several long seconds. As if, he too, were lost in the dwindling fringes of some profundity that had just transpired.

Eventually, he raised his head and looked about the room, as if still thinking. The murmuring of the crowd began to subside, eventually containing itself to a hushed silence that echoed explosively through the room. Everybody awaited in anxious anticipation of what the man was about to say.

I could make out the tell-tale sign of a lavaliere microphone pinned to the lapel of the professor's suit coat, so it was no surprise when Lownsbury's voice boomed through the lecture hall speakers. His gentle, proper, South African, English inflection radiated through the room, delighting the ears of all. But, what he said wasn't exactly what I thought he was going to say.

"How entertaining," he smiled. "Now, there is a group of children that really have something against history class."

The tension had been relieved, and the crowd fell into subdued laughter and applause, eventually, once again, achieving silence.

"Let me share with you what I learned just now," he began.

"For all that we have discovered regarding the history of man, the more we learn how little we actually understand. Mankind's history has repeatedly been forgotten throughout the centuries, for economic reasons, invading armies and, more often than not, as we have just been witness to, a failure of education."

Lownsbury furrowed his brow in thought as he continued speaking; more from immediate consideration than from practice.

"This occurrence has come to be known through the ages as *Collective Amnesia*. A phenomena that repeatedly occurs every few generations.

"Looking at our own American civilization of today, we can now easily understand how the Roman people could lose track of their own systems of governance. And, how the Egyptian people could forget their own empirical lineage.

"Like those mighty civilizations past, our younger generations have now embarked upon their own crusade to wipe clean the memories of this country's history; its successes and its failures.

"It is a sad moment in time when a civilization bends itself to this misguided principle. But, history is replete with unexplainable events. Interesting occurrences. Happenstance that changes the course of the future."

Lownsbury offered a gesture towards the door that the protestors had just been pushed through.

"What we have just been witness to, ladies and gentlemen, is a travesty of our own making. A growing population of people that have little, to no critical decision making capabilities.

"Instead, these masses are governed almost entirely by their emotions. Believing they are pissed about some imagined injustice or another, but having little information as to the truth of the matter.

"And, this too is not a new story."

Lownsbury continued gesturing, "The flamboyant proclamations of the more famous slogans through our recent history include, *'My ancestors were not monkeys!'* or *'You are a fool to believe in God!' 'You are a global warming denier!'*

"These slogans have originated within ephemeral clouds of thoughtless emotion. The speaker understanding virtually nothing of what they are protesting.

"Since time immemorial; through every civilization that has come and gone, young people have proven easy to lead. Thus, the concept of unscrupulous leaders filling our children's heads with emotion based nonsense is not a new story either."

Lownsbury walked towards the edge of the stage as he continued, "I picture these young, ignorant masses as children in the grocery store. Throwing a tantrum over their desire to have a candy bar. Their parent stands idly by, attempting to ignore the child while, at once, cowering before their fellow citizens who stand poised to reveal their barbarism of a child to the nearest authority or *'expert'* should a harsh word be uttered. Eventually, unknowing of what else to do, the parent will acquiesce and buy the unruly child a candy bar.

"This parent, fearing life changing retribution by the so-called *'experts'*," (Lownsbury lifted the two fingers of each hand into the air, fingering the proverbial air quotations each time he said the word *'experts',*) "Leave the parent unsure of what else to do with the spoiled child.

"Yet, nature is informing the parent of what to do. Giving him or her the necessary instinctual behavior of what must be done to educate their children. But, our *'experts'* (again the air quotes) have successfully cowed our parents into thinking that nature is not to be believed and, in fact ignored. And now, our spoiled child has just learned that a temper tantrum will achieve his desires."

Lownsbury drew a heavy breath, continuing, "The single, most important subject in which we need to instruct our children is in our own history. A healthy dose of reading, writing and arithmetic would be icing, of course, but history is where we all learn where we were yesterday, so that we may understand where we are going tomorrow. Not only as individuals, but as a society, a nation, a people. We cannot have a successful future if we do not understand our own past."

Lownsbury cast an evaluating gaze around the audience.

"This simple understanding is evident, even in the actions of the story tellers of civilizations long ago."

Lownsbury was moving easily back and forth across the dais. Expertly engaging the audience with his eloquent dialect.

"One can easily imagine the elders of a small tribe, as they sat around the communal fire, regaling their young with stories of the tribe's experience.

"This instinctual activity, even found in its various forms throughout other areas of the animal kingdom, clearly instructs us that the history of any group is the first, most important lesson that can be instilled in our youth.

"But, our *'experts'* will treat the subject of history cavalierly. As if it were the naive ramblings of an uninformed, past generation of people, not worthy of a second thought."

Lownsbury paused, his eyes traveling over every face.

"There is good reason why our *'experts'* are so quick to disregard, and even disparage our past."

Lownsbury gestured towards the exit doors, and the protestors beyond.

"Rewriting our history for their own political motivations, these *'experts'* will take our adult children, already brimming with unbridled emotion, and fill them full of extraordinary propaganda.

"Relieving them of any remaining filter of critical thought, they then unleash these grown children into our world. Totally ill equipped to face the impact that nature will insist on throwing at them. And now, all of us, as learned adults, have to deal with these grown children and try to teach them right from wrong. And, we know in our hearts that it may be far too late for that."

A small murmur bounced through the hall, quickly subsiding.

Lownsbury nodded thoughtfully, continuing, "It is said that forty is the new thirty. Well twenty would certainly be the new ten, then. At twenty, these ignorant young men and women, never having achieved an adequate education in history, have only the history and experience of being that child in the grocery store."

He lifted his eyes, "Unfortunately, at twenty, the temper tantrum can turn quite violent if they do not think they are being taken seriously. And, that is something we, as the adults, have to prepare for. Because there is no way we can take these children seriously."

Lownsbury paused as he started shaking his head, "Safe space indeed! What meaningless, parochial drivel."

There was laughter of relief against the tension that hung in the air, and even Lownsbury smiled at his own humor.

The man was charming; obviously charismatic, but his eyes continued to affect me with the profound wisdom they seemed to project. At that moment, I would have come to believe him to be an oracle of cultures long past.

"One of my favorite animations are the old *'Looney Tunes',"* Lownsbury resumed with a trace of smile.

There was a small bit of applause at the mention of the old program.

"Well written, thought provoking and irreverent. A perfect instructional tool for our youth."

Lownsbury became a bit more animated as he recounted an anecdote, "I am reminded of one in particular in which an entire tree is felled, and run through a massive machine in a lumber mill where it is chopped and sawed, and at the end, a single toothpick is produced that drops into a box of a hundred such toothpicks."

There was a short burst of applause and laughter as many in the group remembered the sketch.

Lownsbury continued, "We as critical thinkers can look at that cartoon and realize it for what it is. A dramatized interpretation of the undeniable wastefulness of man. It is funny for the element of truth it contains."

He shook his head, his voice dropping dramatically, "But, it is not literal truth.

"These young, passionate people outside those doors," he gestured, "Could look at that animation as a direct interpretation. Unable to filter it through critical thought to realize it for the parody it is, they would perhaps view it as a literal construct. Each of these children may come to believe that all of us, in this room, will leave here tonight and eradicate an entire acre of trees because our toothpick supply is dwindling."

Subdued laughter through the crowd, devolved into restless murmuring and eventual silence.

"Instinctively, those grown children know something is not right with our society. Just as we too realize it.

"But, with only the mentality of a child, and with no historical reference or education to guide them, they have no idea of what the underlying issue is, or how to correct it. So, their emotions take hold and a tantrum ensues."

Murmurs of appreciation and nods of approval drifted through the hall.

"We, as seasoned adults, understand the problem in a different way. We attempt to explain to our youth what the problems are through our understanding of history and how our ancestors lived through these same afflictions. But, our rational ideas, often times, fall to deaf emotional ears. They cannot understand our concepts of critical thinking, and the tantrum is often turned towards us."

Still moving across the dais.

"This inability to communicate with each other becomes the reason for societies failures and, eventually, civilization collapse.

"And, this too, is not a new story."

A pause.

"These are the youth of our future, ladies and gentlemen, and of our eventual demise. Excited with the purposeful backing of a handful of our *'experts'*, our new era of *Collective Amnesia* is well underway."

Someone from the crowd shouted something. I could not hear distinctly what was said, but Doctor Lownsbury reiterated.

"Self-fulfilling prophecy? Likely. Nature whispers to us what we need to do. And, as a people, we insist, rarely, if ever, on listening.

"But, even this too is nature at work. The distinct nature of man. And, it is these elements of nature and the defined nature of man that we will be delving into during the duration of this lecture. An encapsulation of our unique *Syndromes of Civilization.*"

Several members of the audience suddenly began to filter up on stage. Taking a position behind Lownsbury. Apparent volunteers for a demonstration that was undoubtedly forthcoming. Guided along by the usher, they stood about in a loose grouping.

Lownsbury ignored them as he continued addressing the audience.

"As we prepare to construct our civilization, the first and most profound thing to address as to the undeniable nature of man, and what creates his distinction in the animal kingdom, is our capability for defining our spirituality."

Lownsbury paused as his eyes roamed the faces of all that were there.

"We are spiritual beings," he continued, "Whether we all realize it or not. Whether we all agree to it or not. We are spiritual. It is inarguable.

"Part of how we seek that spirituality is our seemingly blind faith in certain concepts. Namely, science and religion. Science and religion are merely two sides of the same coin, a token. and we call that token, *faith*."

Lownsbury's gate was purposeful, his eyes penetrating. I was certain each member of the audience could feel the power he was projecting.

"Spirituality can be defined as the recognition that there is something bigger than ourselves. That we are not the top of the food chain. That there is something far larger than ourselves that cannot be taken for granted.

"Its name has changed through the years. Many of us are inclined to refer to it as Mother Nature.

"Some prefer to give it a direct consciousness by calling it God. And, I see no reason to argue that point. For I am not inclined to find any evidence to the contrary."

Applause of approval filtered through the hall.

"Some call this force, *instinct*," Lownsbury continued, "Some simply call it *'The Force'*."

A few knowing chuckles drifted through the audience and even Lownsbury's eyes seemed to twinkle at the reference.

"The crucial thing to realize though, is that the force of nature is there and we understand that it is immovable to us. That we exist at its mercy."

The professor enunciated the next few words with emotion, *"This is the basis of man's spirituality."*

His eyes blazed around the room, casting up to the balcony and diving to the back row. An energy emanated within him and I could feel it as his eyes came to rest on me.

"There are, however, our typical handful of *'experts'*, just like those that presume to tell us all how to live, that will exclaim that we are the kings of our domain and that we hold dominion over these forces of nature," he said.

"Again, an old story.

"It is these false prophets, as they used to be called, these *'experts'*, that lie and deceive us. That tell us we can control that force. That we can control *God*, if you will.

"But, if these so-called experts, that I call *Rain Makers,* are to be believed, we would certainly lose our spirituality and create a vacuum in which another religion or science can fill that vacancy.

"This misguided manner of thinking I refer to as, ***The Rain Maker Syndrome***. Which I will explain in due course."

Lownsbury's eyes softened, "But, even with our arrogant struggles we mount against nature, we are ironically, still giving in to nature's demands. The fight *we* mount against nature, is a fight *we*, as humans, can never win.

Two

The Society

A restroom break had been called and none too soon. Although, rather than make for the nearest facility, I felt compelled to meet face to face with Professor Lownsbury. His eyes, even from such a distance, were having a profound effect on me. The shadowy hints of epiphany I had been experiencing only seemed to enhance the need to meet him. It seemed essential that I see him up close.

He was talking to his handful of volunteers, offering them instructions and adhesive name tags that could be stuck to their clothing. They were huddled around him, obviously thrilled with the prospect of being assistants to his lecture.

He was fully engaged with his volunteers, but when I approached, he seemed to know I was there and his gaze traveled up to meet mine. A trace of a knowing smile spread across his face.

I was instantly captivated. His eyes were like none I had ever encountered. Deep, and incisive. That feeling of epiphany I had been experiencing all evening returned with a force.

I was becoming increasingly disoriented, but I managed to stumble through a few words of greeting as I clumsily offered my hand.

"It is an honor to meet you, Doctor Lownsbury," I heard myself say.

Lownsbury held my gaze for several long seconds, his eyes penetrating into my soul. It were as if he was able to see right through me. A slight upturn of his lip was followed by his own hand grasping mine.

"How serendipitous," he said.

His greeting was warm, and sincere. Yet, somewhat awkward and incomplete. His handshake was firm, abrupt. I had been in the presence of celebrity many times during the course of my career, but this had been the first time I had actually felt star-struck.

No further words were uttered and I took his leave feeling a bit foolish over my callow approach. But, I was increasingly confused at Professor Lownsbury's greeting, as well.

"Serendipitous," he had said.

What had he meant by that?

I ran the conversation, such as it was, through my memory, searching for some meaning behind his strange recipience. But, I could find no frame of reference in which he may have chosen to respond in that manner.

Serendipitous.

I had not had the presence of mind in the moment to ask him what he meant, and now the moment had passed.

I breathed a heavy sigh as I tried to clear my confusion over Professor Lownsbury's odd mannerism.

Serendipitous.

I managed to return to my seat just as order was called again, and I turned my attention to the program that had been handed me when I had first entered the hall.

Inside the program, I found several sheets of printed material.

This was the first:

SOCIETY

PRODUCERS:

GOODS; Tangible
Gary: Makes tools and weapons
Greg: Delivers Food (Hunter/ Gatherer, Farmer)
Gwen: Delivers raw materials, (Wood, Ore, Gems, etc)

SERVICES; Intangible
Sam: Engineer (Designer, Inventor, Creator) (Mind)
Sue: Laborer (Physical, Manufacturing) (Body)
Sylvia: Cooks (Anything from wine to meals) (Soul)

TOKENS:

Phil: *Philosopher*, (Teachers, Scientists, Press, Authors) Anybody that describes our world and ourselves to us through thought and emotion.

Tom: *Thief* (One side of token Hero, other side Villain) Job is to steal the property of another for their benefactor, or themselves.

Rule-Maker: One side is Politician, flip side is Clergy. Both sides bicker or work together for the ***control*** of Producers property.

Doug: *Dreg*. His Existence is exemplified with the harboring of mankind's ***Seven Deadly Sins***. Dregs are multi-faceted because so many Producers and Tokens will drift in and out of the Dregs. Most of our Rule-Makers are pulled from this category.

As the crowd once again fell to silence, Doctor Lownsbury's focus seemed to energize.

"Since the first medicine man convinced his neighbor to feed him for his magical insight and abilities, and the first toolmaker displayed his wares to his fellow man, mankind has existed with the same instinct for survival as he does today."

Lownsbury began his easy shuffle across the dais, engaging every member of his audience.

"The question we now ask is, How does this manifest itself?

"Let's take it back to the beginning. As a logical thinking people, everything can be taken to its base beginning. Narrowed into a microcosm. Let's focus down to the most easy to understand mechanism in which we can look at our societies today.

"Let us first talk about the *Meaning of Life* and how we define that concept."

Someone in the audience shouted, *"Forty two!"* which brought a few chuckles of those who understood the Douglas Adams reference.

Lownsbury merely offered a semblance of a smile and a nod of his head as he continued.

"Everybody wants to know the meaning of life," he said, "But, it is really not hard to understand.

"The meaning of our individual lives is the acquisition of property. Of belongings. If we suddenly materialized into the middle of nowhere, naked with nothing. Our first goal would be the acquisition of protection from the elements in the form of shelter and clothing, and then food.

"Once those items are acquired, it would then be the further and ongoing acquirement of tools and other property to make our lives easier in the ongoing acquisition of further property.

"This property acquisition would also include companionship, and community, for the purposes of survival, emotional fulfillment, and procreation.

"Since our meaning of life has been defined as the acquirement of property, let us now state the definition of property."

Lownsbury walked back to the large board that had been divided into three sections. Pulling back the cloth that had been covering the first section of the white board, Lownsbury revealed what was written beneath.

*"**PROPERTY**: That which a person possesses, Tangible or Intangible, that can be traded or otherwise bartered in the acquisition of another person's property, Tangible or Intangible."*

Lownsbury read the words, then offered a raised eyebrow back to the audience, "Tangible, or Intangible. Let us further define those terms."

Pulling aside another cloth on the second third of the white board, he revealed.

*"**Tangible:** Physical items that can be held and put to a constructive use. A material object."*

Lownsbury again read the words as he pointed to objects on the dais, "The definition is pretty obvious and would, no doubt include items such as a table or chair. But, how about this?"

Lownsbury reached into his pocket and pulled forth a dollar bill, displaying it to the audience.

"This can be possessed, traded, used. It can be taken from us as retribution or punishment. By our definition, it is indeed our personal property."

Nods and agreement issued forth from the audience.

"For now, let us include money as a part of our property."

Lownsbury pointed to the other word on the board, reading again.

*"**Intangible:** This is where we include our time; A persons Mind, Body, and Soul."*

Lownsbury brought the fingers of his right hand together as he enunciated his next words, "This definition includes our very lives."

He took a visible breath inside of a heavy pause before continuing.

"I want to make a special point around the consideration of our soul as property.

"The acquisition of companionship is how we fulfill our souls. It is how we keep it healthy. Our soul is where our passions reside, and it contains our own unique way of how we define and express ourselves."

Lownsbury was speaking now with a great deal of intensity; enunciating, with animation, each word. His manner was captivating, and all ears and eyes were focused on him.

"Our souls are manifest in the way we interact with each other. In the emotions we feel, and the love we promote and desire. It is our property. And, it can be lost, or bartered."

He paused again, looking around the room.

"We have all heard of the term, *'Trading one's soul for power or glory'*. It is a euphemistic terminology for those, that in the acquisition of the power they achieved, lost a part of themselves along the way. Degenerating into a darkness that kept them from keeping their souls healthy, and alive."

The audience responded with an eerie quiet for several long seconds until Lownsbury again broke the stillness.

"I have asked a number of the audience to join me on stage," his professorial demeanor returning. "They will be our representatives of our society we will build. I will introduce them all to you, one by one."

Lownsbury smiled, "Society begins with one person."

Lownsbury gestured and a short balding man from the group of volunteers behind him, approached.

"This is Gary, alone in the wilderness."

Although Gary had not made a move otherwise, Lownsbury grabbed his arm, "No, Gary, keep your pants on. You do not need to be naked, too. Your acquisition of clothing has been presumed."

There was laughter that radiated through the room, eventually subsiding.

I was finding Lownsbury's lecture entertaining and rewarding thus far, and was still questioning my peers' motivations for decrying my desire to attend.

Again, that intense feeling of an epiphany, drifting just outside my reach, lay its persistent, feathered touch upon me. I breathed deep, my mind alert.

On the dais, Lownsbury handed Gary a small woven basket.

"Gary is a tool and textile maker. His basket contains a small representation of a blanket. Gary makes tangible items to be traded. He can weave baskets and mold clay. His arrows are straight and fly true."

Lownsbury grabbed Gary's arm with direction, "Gary, close your eyes, extend your arms. Now spin in a short circle."

As Gary did what he was instructed, Lownsbury explained, "This, my friends, is absolute freedom. Gary can spin as free, as fast, and as blind as he chooses. Within this one person, there is absolute freedom."

Lownsbury again grabbed for Gary's arm.

"Ok, that's enough. Please, take a seat right here. Thank you."

Lownsbury directed the man to a row of six chairs that had been set along stage right. The row of chairs were separated down the middle; three on each side. Slightly askew as to face each other, yet still facing the audience. He directed Gary to the first chair on the left side.

"But, Gary is not as effective in his life by himself as he could be with someone else. Human beings are a social animal, as we all know."

Lownsbury gestured for his next guest, and a short, rather homely, young black lady walked out and stood next to Lownsbury.

"This is Sam. Sam is an inventor. An engineer."

Taking her basket that Lownsbury handed her, she reached into it and produced a small compass, displaying it to the audience with a shy smile.

"She makes work with the use of her mind. She can think of anything and how to create it. However, as she joins Gary in his social construct, she tells him: If you want to spin with your arms outstretched, you can no longer do it with your eyes closed."

Taking a marker to the smaller white board on wheels, Lownsbury wrote the word, *'Rules'* along the top.

Midway down the board he made a small vertical hash mark. Remarking, "Our first rule. *'We will not harm each other'.*"

Lownsbury turned, "Gary no longer has absolute freedom. Neither one of them do. In order for two or more people to live together in a society, there must be some form of rules for them to associate with each other. It is an absolute necessity, and it represents the end of absolute freedom."

Lownsbury directed Sam to the first chair on the right side.

Lownsbury then walked over to Gary, already seated and put a hand on his shoulder.

"Gary represents Goods. Products. Our *Tangible* forms of property."

Lownsbury then walked over to Sam. Placing a hand on her shoulder.

"Sam represents Services. These are our *Intangible* items."

"G... Gary, G... Goods. S... Sam. S...Services. I trust you see the pattern. I have renamed our people for this experiment. It helps me keep things straight."

Gentle laughter echoed through the hall, quickly subsiding. Lownsbury was proving rather amusing.

"Gary has decided that since Sam has the ability to make a rule they must follow, he would like to create a rule as well. Gary insists that they will remember their history and keep the honor of their ancestors alive by teaching their wisdom to the young."

Lownsbury made another random mark in the field of the white board.

"Behind these two will reside the representations of those of us throughout society that fall into these two categories, Goods and Services. Each representing our property to be bartered.

"Behind Gary, we will have Greg."

Lownsbury gestured and another volunteer came to stage center to stand with him. He was tall and wore glasses. He sported a tie but had discarded his coat in deference to the warmth of the room. His skin was a deeper shade of black than Lownsbury's or Sam's.

Lownsbury handed him a basket.

"Greg is a hunter and gatherer."

Greg reached into his basket and withdrew a plastic knife, displaying it to the audience.

"He provides meat and berries to our little tribe in the making. He is an expert in providing the necessary sustenance. However, he has a rule of his own: Greg will tell the rest of his tribe not to shout and make useless noise for fear of scaring away the game."

Lownsbury approached his white board and made another random hash mark. *"We will not shout useless epithets."*

Turning back to the audience, Lownsbury drew a breath.

"Greg trades portions of his meat to Gary for quivers of arrows. He also trades with Sam for designing a smokehouse to cure his meat. Please take a seat next to Gary. Thank you."

Greg sat in the designated seat.

Lownsbury gestured to another volunteer as he reached into his stash of baskets. Another young lady stepped forward. She was middle aged but quite striking. Her hair was shoulder length and a beautiful auburn color.

"Over here we have Sue. Sue is a laborer."

Reaching into her basket she revealed a child's plastic hammer.

"Sue can build anything. She can hammer a nail and she can dig a hole. She is the labor behind every effort. She represents one of the most important groups of people in our history. Sue's profession's have shaped our world and how we live.

"Greg asks Sue to build the smokehouse that Sam designed. And for her efforts, she shares a portion of meat. But, Sam has a rule too; she explains that she will not work one day out of the week."

As Lownsbury made another vertical mark on the white board, he remarked, "Sue has created a day of rest for the group, an important rule for the health of everyone's body and soul. Please take a seat behind Sam, if you will. Thank you."

Sue stepped toward stage right as Lownsbury produced another basket and motioned for another volunteer to join him. A tall woman, equally striking as Sue stepped forward. Her blonde hair hung near her waist.

"Behind Greg, we have Gwen. What is in your basket Gwen?"

Gwen reached in her basket and pulled out a small plastic saw as could be found in a child's play tool kit.

"Gwen is a miner. A lumberjack. She provides the group all of the raw materials they need to perform their functions of cooking, of building. She may have Sue help her fell a tree, and Sue will in turn take a significant portion of lumber to construct her projects.

"Gwen also has a rule. She keeps a very tight inventory of the trees she has felled and the rocks she has unearthed. She demands that nobody take the materials she works very hard to acquire without her knowledge."

Lownsbury made another hash mark on the white board, remarking, *"Nobody steals from each other."* He gestured, "Please take that last seat on the left side behind Gary and Greg. Thank you, Gwen."

Lownsbury reached for another basket with his left hand as he motioned with his right. He handed the basket to a woman, likely in her mid thirties. She was plump, but not unattractive. Her clothes were not as fancy as Sue's were, but they were not shabby either.

"Finally, we have Sylvia. Sylvia is a cook."

Sylvia pulled a plastic spatula from her basket and displayed it to the audience.

"We need somebody to brew our beer, make our wine, and discover the best preparations of our meals. She tends the fire and makes sure we are all fed. She is a butcher, and herb preparer.

"Sylvia insists that the meat Greg delivers is properly smoked and cured. Her rule is: *that the talk around the dinner table not be one of gossip.*"

Lownsbury made another mark on his board. The marks appeared arbitrary within the field he was making them. I was curious where he was going to take this random course. I figured I would soon find out.

"We now have six people out of ten in our society. We call them *'The Producers'*. They trade their goods and services with each other. They have a nice little economy going. Greg can exchange his bows and arrows to any member, and in exchange, he is fed. He can have a tool shed designed and built, and each of the members of this commune can benefit from each other's efforts.

"We have our people and those that will line up behind them as *Goods;* or tangible property to be traded. And, *Services;* our intangible property. This will include; *Mind, Body, and Soul.*"

Lownsbury stepped over and gestured to Sam Sue and Sylvia, respectively, as he said the words, "*Mind Body and Soul.*"

"Our growing population will come in varieties of subsets of these groups we have here. Our cooks may become cafe owners, and Brew Masters. Vintners. Delivering their services with love.

"Greg's underlings will grow into farmers and store merchants. Each of our Producers will provide the necessary sustenance for a society."

"But, now as our society is growing, there are some issues that need resolved. We find we need another set of professionals, we call *'The Tokens'*."

Lownsbury approached a stand. It looked much like a microphone stand, but instead of a microphone clip, it sported a wire frame loop at the top that held a representation of a coin. The coin was a simple laminated poster board about the diameter of a large platter. Displaying it on both sides, Lownsbury showed green colored poster board on one side, and red on the other. He placed this stand holding the *Token* in front of two chairs that occupied stage left.

Lownsbury continued in stride, "The two sides of our Tokens will have respective job descriptions that share similar definitions. Many times the two opposing sides will have similar mindsets which means that they may become interchangeable. Only certain distinctions place them on their respective sides of the coin. I will explain this further as we go along."

Motioning, basket already in hand, Lownsbury called another one of the three remaining volunteers to join him. He was a tall thin man, as tall as Lownsbury. He wore wire rimmed glasses and parted his thin hair to the side.

"Our first Token is our Philosopher. This is Phil.

"Philosophers are people who observe the world around us and the people that we are. They bring those observations to us, and they can do that through *Reason*."

Lownsbury motioned to the poster board coin, displaying the green side.

"Or, through our *Emotions*."

Lownsbury flipped the stand around and displayed the red side of the Token.

"The Philosophers instruct us as to who we are and our place in this world. They do not have to be correct, in fact they are frequently incorrect. But, many times we mistakenly view their words as gospel. For instance, our group of so called *'experts',* that we have pilloried at the onset of our demonstration here, are also a member of this group of philosophers.

"I place those aforementioned *'experts'* on the side of *Emotions*. They instruct us all on how the world should be, at times in deference to nature, and not necessarily on how the world really is.

"Our goal as Producers should not be to believe these Philosophers out of hand. That would be foolish. But, we should always take their observations and evaluate them through our own filters of critical thought. A skeptical analysis, to determine for ourselves what is worthy of further consideration. Some of these Philosophers, as we have learned, deserve no further attention.

"These Philosophers come in a variety of forms. They are our teachers, our scientists and doctors. But, they are also our actors and comedians, our journalists and authors."

I found myself feeling a bit sheepish at being a part of the group Lownsbury was discussing. Yet, also rather justified in my attitude towards my grumbling colleagues. I had not considered this avenue of thinking concerning my profession before, but I realized just how profound the professor seemed to be in his assessment.

Lownsbury continued, "Phil becomes part of our social construct, but because he is a Token, he is not considered a Producer. He may have a service to offer, but it is in the form of ideas. Of existentialism. His goal is to attempt persuasion, but his words may not have an ounce of truth to them, other than perhaps to Phil, himself. If our children can learn from Phil, even if it is merely critical thinking against what Phil is teaching, then he has done his job."

"Many Philosophers enjoy the stage and have tremendous egos. They love the camera and the limelight, although they rarely like it shown in a dissenting manner on their work.

"Rarely does anyone enjoy criticism, but the Philosopher's ego rarely allow for any dissent at all.

"Philosophers are not Producers. Their attempts at persuasion can, at times, be emotion based. So, our Producers do not allow them to set any rules, themselves. But, rules can be made for them.

"Therefore our Producers decide to create a rule on Phil's behalf. In order to keep their tremendous vanity in check, there will be no statues or awards given to our Philosophers. They can bring us their ideas that we deem worthy. But, we will not place them upon apotheosized pedestals. They are simply men and women like us."

Lownsbury made another large mark in a seemingly random area of the board of rules.

I suddenly had an understanding of the rules Lownsbury was creating. They were the Ten Commandments in a very basic form. An easy to understand, secular format that made it clear as to why a growing civilization would need those basic tenets.

The rule concerning Phil was obviously against creating graven images. Sue insisted on remembering the Sabbath. While Gary's rule was to honor their ancestors by instructing the youth of their society's history. It seemed so simple as to why these commandments had come into existence, and why they were so important. Lownsbury was indeed a master at his craft, and I was appreciating every minute.

Lownsbury waved over another volunteer with a call of his name, "Tom."

A beefy looking guy strode to center stage and accepted the basket Lownsbury offered him. He was a good looking guy with the body of someone who spent a good deal of time in the gym.

"Our next Token is the Thief. Tom is our Thief.

"Now, I want to be very clear," Lownsbury stressed, "A Thief, regardless of the negative connotations imagined with the use of that term, is not necessarily a bad thing. Even though his job description is literally to steal the property of Producers and others. Although not necessarily the property of our Producers behind me. At least at this moment in time.

"At this moment in our society, if Tom is working at the behest of our Producers to steal the property of his counterpart, *"The Villains,"* he is considered a soldier or hero.

"If he is working only for himself he is considered the criminal or villain. Both sides of his coin share a similar mentality."

Lownsbury pointed back towards Phil, "Whereas Phil tends towards a mentality that his ideas and emotions are supreme above and beyond that of the Producers, Tom tends towards a consideration that he is above the law."

"Both of these Tokens, the Philosopher and the Thief, like the Producers, work for the benefit of a benefactor. They work with his best interest in mind. Perhaps Greg over here has heard that the nearby village has a new kind of axe that is easier to wield or stays sharper longer, and he wants Tom to go spy on the village and steal the new axe.

"Or, Sylvia hears rumors that the neighboring village has a killer recipe for pork chops. Tom can be hired by the Producers to procure those items.

"His job would also be that of defense. He knows how to fight, and will help protect his community from the neighboring village Thief.

"Tom has inspired a rule too. The wives of the Producer's love a strong man. Warriors, be they Hero's or Villains, have always held a fascination with women. Much the same way that feminine characteristics do with men. A hot beef cake is always an enticement, and as such, the Producers create yet another rule.

"We will keep our marital bed sacrosanct. A woman needs a man to help her care for their offspring, and both sides would naturally fear diseases which would certainly have been known. As husband and wife, our society simply agrees and makes a promise not to cheat on each other. Marriage is thereby, created."

Lownsbury made another mark. By now it was easy to decipher the rules the professor was espousing. It was also easy to see why such rules would have come into existence.

"Tom and Phil, as we mentioned, are beholden to their Producers. The Producers feed and house our two Tokens for the work they perform, and this relationship is symbiotic.

"This brings us to a very important point that needs to be addressed."

Tom took a seat next to Phil, stage left, as Lownsbury continued.

"In our current society, many of us have been conditioned to think that self-employed people are somehow privileged. That they make a massive amount of money and crawl into beds filled with hundred dollar bills to fall asleep at night."

Lownsbury took a deep breath within a long pause.

He resumed, "Something we need to always remember ladies and gentlemen. We are all self-employed, each of us. Some of us desire to work at our own system. To seek out our clients on our own terms and to set our schedules to our own desires.

"Others choose to have someone else set the organization and rules for us. They prefer to show up at a particular time, and go home when the shift is over. For those of us that choose to have only one client; an employer, we take a lower amount of pay. As part of that convenience, we do not have to market ourselves constantly. We do not have to wonder where our next job will come from. We still charge what we think our time is worth, or what the market will allow. But, not to the degree we would if we had to hustle constantly for our next meal.

"Regardless of whether we work exclusively for that one client, or many clients, like the so called, self employed, it's important to remember: *Each of us, are all beholden to that person who signs our paycheck.*"

Lownsbury enunciated these last words with hand movements on each syllable.

He ended, "I call this the *Benefactor Principle*."

This was a thought I had not considered before. The professor was giving me new things to think about, but I also was curious as to why he enunciated this point so strongly.

"As our group continues to grow," Professor Lownsbury continued, "Our Producers have decided to come together and provide for our two Tokens for the benefit of the entire group. Sam designs a school house that Sue constructs while Sylvia continues to provide meals.

"Phil the Teacher, instructs our Producer's children according to his clients desires, which first and foremost contains the group's history.

"Tom protects all of them from harm, and the members of our community work towards the benefit of each other. Each providing their services in kind to the other.

"Our two Tokens are beholden to the rest of the group; their benefactors, because that is how they are sustained. They will perform their finest efforts in the interest of the Producers because that is who they owe their allegiance. No one else."

Lownsbury offered a long pause, taking a sip of water from his glass before continuing.

"Before I introduce our ninth person in this social construct, I want to talk about our commune."

Lownsbury began his familiar idle pacing across the dais.

"Our commune is just that. A near perfect form of communism.

"I wish to make a distinction to all of you. This community is not one of *'What's yours is mine, and what's mine is yours.'* That form of communism never works. It doesn't work with siblings, it certainly doesn't work as a community. We all enjoy our own possessions. Our own personal property.

"As we determined, the acquisition of property, in its various forms, is the meaning of life for most of us. This idea of shedding our personal belongings and sharing the fruits of our labor freely with others is an unsustainable concept. Even those select few that follow that pipe dream are so rare that, even if they engage in it for any length of time, are so much the exception to the rule as to be ignored.

"Typically, these select few, as with many of us, desire the realization of absolute freedom. But, as long as other people exist in our world, there can no longer be absolute freedom. These simple few who wish to live in that form of commune will, many times, consider the ownership of private property the antithesis of freedom, but will still strive to obtain a certain amount of property for themselves, nonetheless. Whether its food, or shelter. Or, even a simple corkscrew.

"Although, some may just prefer that the Producers provide for them," he smiled.

"Remember, the meaning of life is the acquisition of property. It is the symbol of freedom for most of us, and so we will not consider that particular, romanticized idea of communal living as valid for our demonstration.

"Nor, do I want this confused with socialist communism, defined as military enforced, governmental oppression of a society. Our commune is a *voluntary* form of living. Without the formation of government. It is everyone *selfishly* working with each other for the benefit of the whole community, while maintaining control of their own property."

This was a concept I had not considered. Communism voluntary? Selfish? I was by now writing furiously in an attempt to capture all of Lownsbury's words. Kicking myself for not having the presence of mind to have turned on the voice recorder of my phone. My fingers stumbled across the phone's screen in between my frantic scribbling.

"In other words," Lownsbury was moving across the dais in that easy gait I had come to recognize, "To selfishly work for the benefit of everyone in society, can be further defined as the desire to be compensated for the use of your property in the bartering, trade or acquisition of someone else's property."

Lownsbury stopped middle stage and touched his fingertips together.

"Let me say that again:

"It is the desire to be compensated for the use of your property; your life and your worldly goods. In the bartering, trade or acquisition of someone else's property."

A slight pause, "Sue will not build tables for Sylvia to use, if Sylvia will not make any meals. Sylvia has to provide her services in kind. There can be no room for sloth if a community is to survive."

Lownsbury began his casual pacing again.

"But, our ninth person is not wholly welcome in our commune. At least at this moment in time. He exists, but only on the outer fringes.

"Our ninth person is what I call a Multi-faceted Token. And, this Token we call *The Dreg.*"

Lownsbury motioned and the remaining volunteer walked over. He was offered a basket, but it was shown to be empty.

The young man, his hair a bit long and draped across the corner of his left eye, smiled and shrugged his shoulders.

"Doug is our Dreg of society.

"Of all the forms of nature that man either embraces or denies, philosophers throughout many civilizations argued that our emotions should always remain suspect. It has long been considered that the mastery of our emotions was that singular trait that would raise the human being above the rest of the animal kingdom.

"For emotions can change or be molded based upon experiences. Our emotions can be used against us or even manipulated in order to appease a manipulator."

Lownsbury gestured towards the exterior door. Obviously referring to the children outside.

"Therefore, past generations of mankind have determined that major decisions and the manner in which we conduct our lives should not be based upon those emotions. And, more importantly, personal traits that are inherent in all of us, traits spawned from our emotions, were considered taboo."

Lownsbury paused as he took another sip from his water glass. The usher appeared, as if by magic, and swapped Lownsbury's now empty glass with a fresh one.

The professor resumed, "But, certainly not all of our emotions should be included in that rule, should they?" he asked resuming his purposeful pace. "I mean, our emotions are such a factor in who we are and what we believe, we cannot simply dismiss them, should we?"

Lownsbury shook his head, and smiled.

"So our ancient philosophers divided the most destructive of the human traits, spawned by our base emotions, into seven distinct forms. Seven unique characteristics that should be avoided in order for a civilization to exist. And, for a people to live in peace with one another."

Lownsbury looked to his volunteer and back to the audience.

"And Doug, as a multi-faceted Token Dreg of our society, embodies all seven of these distinct characteristics. He not only displays these aspects in his day to day life, but also engenders inside the rest of us, those seven deadly sins."

Lownsbury spread his hands.

"In other words, Doug ensures our society does not stagnate in the mire of prosperity."

Micro-bursts of laughter ignited randomly through the hall, and I saw the trace of a smile cross Lownsbury's face.

"Let's look at these seven distinct traits and how they encompass our lives. These seven characteristics are no secret. We all know them, and they of course include Gluttony, Greed, Pride, Lust, Wrath, Sloth and Envy. Each of these individual sins are categorized under a single umbrella we call *self-indulgence.*

"Dregs are unique people and a good portion of their population is made up of Producer's dabbling with the described characteristics; being self-indulgent from time to time. But, there are a number of people that have chosen to make a career as a Dreg. I will mention just a few that seem to remain fully entrenched within the Dregs, and I always like to begin with gluttony."

A brief pause as Lownsbury seemed to consider his next words.

"Clowns are one of my favorite kinds of people," he said matter-of-factly, "Clowns do not necessarily have to be entertainers, but they are usually entertaining to look at," he said. "They consist of those that wish to remove themselves from conventional society. Their dress is designed to repel or thwart convention. If we were to witness, for example, a person walking down the street with strange clothing, oddly colored and sculpted hair and self-inflicted facial deformities; that would be considered the very definition of a clown."

Lownsbury raised his eyebrows as he cast his gaze around the audience.

"Would it not?"

The inevitable murmuring of the crowd quickly subsided.

"Clowns are self-created, non-conventionalists. and the product of pride and gluttony. Often, they will display the attitude of entitlement, and will, many times be of the opinion that society owes them for merely gracing us with their existence. Not a hard and fast rule, but typically, the more garish their appearance, the deeper they are driven by their emotions."

Often times, the richer a society becomes, the more time is available in where people can engage in self-indulgent forms of behavior. And, clowns are among the most self-indulgent among us.

Nods of assent were seen as many began to relate the characteristics with those in their lives of whom they were familiar.

"Lawyers, politicians and money handlers will often represent Greed in a society. And, not surprisingly, this is also the pool from which we pull many of our Rule-Makers.

"Often times, the Greedy create a false need among Producers for self-serving purposes. They will capitalize on injury, whether real or imagined. They are the masters at spreading the seven sins among the Producers for their own purposes and, most importantly, to perpetuate the Dreg.

"In fact, if it weren't for the Greed's perpetuation of the Dregs' traits, the Producers would likely have little need for Greed's services.

"The Greedy are masters at spreading Envy among the populace. They work hard to expand the roles and population of the Dregs. They realize that the Dregs are their life bread and the perpetual proliferation of the Dreg is Greed's ideal."

Lownsbury paused as his eyes passed over the many faces present. "Try to let that sink in for a moment, I said a mouthful and have to give my tongue a rest."

Laughter stretched for several long seconds until Lownsbury, after taking a long pull of water, smiled and continued, "Lust is a unique category. It appeals to everyone to a certain degree from time to time. And, as a result, mostly consists of people from every other walk of life dabbling in this group. Even ladies and gentlemen of the evening can be considered Producers that dabble as Dregs. Their services straddling that line between a deadly sin, and a singular necessity.

"Some will say that Lust encompasses those that self-identify by their sexual proclivities rather than a more noble trait or profession.

But I view Lust in a unique way. I believe the deadly sin that our ancients refer to is the morality of society, as dictated by our women, and the degradation of those ethics and principles.

"Some view these ethics and principles as a puritanical adherence to an outdated belief system.

"In other words, they are viewed as rules made by people that just want to stifle our good time."

Mild laughter quickly abated.

"But, there was a reason for this category of Lust as a deadly sin and the belief that it should be abhorred, and just like the other categories of deadly sins, it had everything to do with survival of the species."

As murmuring and questions erupted through the crowd, Lownsbury held up a hand.

"Please everyone, we will have a question and answer session towards the end, if you don't mind saving your questions until then, it will help things move much more smoothly."

The unintelligible group noise quickly fell to silence.

"Thank you," Lownsbury continued, "Bums, of course, are the epitome of Sloth, although they, too, do not have exclusivity to that title. The Sloth is defined as existing solely on the generosity of the Producers. Most often the Sloth does not provide a good or service in kind. Sloth is the most prolific of the seven traits. Although, not a hard and fast rule, the Sloth often suffers from maladies that can range from mental to physical deformity."

Lownsbury raised his chin and scratched at the stubble, "As I mentioned, many of our Producers or Tokens can dabble as a Dreg from time to time.

"For example: A Producer may have a daughter that actually has a job, but mires herself in self-indulgence by portraying herself as a clown in order to skirt convention.

"And, as I just mentioned, ladies of the evening are actual Producers that dabble in Lust. Or, a successful businessman that wishes to identify himself according to his nocturnal proclivities.

"One of the key elements in the many facets of the career Dreg that they all hold in common, is the self-indulgence aspect. Because of this, they can all be considered untrustworthy members of society.

"Most of the deadly sins that are attributed to the Dregs, were created because it was determined very early in man's history, that the more prolific this group became, the more that the signs of the end of a civilization were near.

"Think of it this way, ladies and gentlemen. As a general rule, the Dregs, which consist largely of Producers dabbling briefly in this arena, should comprise no more than ten percent of the entire population at any given time.

"Each sub group, the greed, sloth, lust, and so forth, manifesting itself as only a fraction of that number.

"If the Dregs were to stretch the boundaries of the ten percent, then they become an arbiter of societal collapse. If the seven deadly sins were to become prolific, then society would become chaotic and population decline would be the result. At least until the traits of the Dregs could be forced back into their proper percentile.

"This is why the Seven sins of the Dregs have always been preached against; for the benefit of the society at large.

"Doug will sit over here on his own."

Lownsbury directed him to a lone chair, situated in front of a grouping of chairs, stage left.

"His Token will represent that of Sloth on one side, and Perfidious, or untrustworthy member of society, on the other.

The Dreg and, as we mentioned, particularly the Sloth, is highly prolific and will typically seek out their own prosperity in deceitful manners and selfish pursuits. Therefore, Doug does not get to set a rule, but as with the other Tokens, one will be made for him."

Lownsbury made another seemingly random mark on the *"Rules"* board, commenting, *"The Dregs will not begrudge what the Producers and Tokens earn."*

I made a mental note; this represented the commandment against coveting, and made a great deal of sense. There was only one more commandment to be made, I calculated, and was curious as to how Lownsbury would represent it.

"You will notice behind Doug there are several chairs lined up."

Lownsbury motioned to several young women I had not noticed before. They were seated near the front row and entrance to the stage on Doug's side of the dais. It was obvious they had purposely been seated in that location by the usher.

"Young ladies, each time you hear this bell ring,"

Lownsbury demonstrated by tapping the small push button bell on his table. It sounded with a solid ding that resonated through the hall.

"I want one of you, one at a time, to come up on stage and take a seat behind Doug."

Lownsbury turned his attention to the audience.

"Our society is now the epitome of near economic perfection, but there are a few of our members that are having some issues."

Lownsbury walked over to the Producers, and gestured as he spoke.

"Gary has decided he wants Sue to work on a project. However, Sue has no need for what Gary is offering. She has no need for any further tools, but she does need some lumber.

"This inequality of trade can be overlooked for a while, but, eventually, it will become a point of contention.

"So, the time has come that Gary needs to go to Greg, to barter for some lumber, in order to procure the services of Sue.

"But, what Greg desires is a jug of homemade wine in trade. Gary then has to go to Sylvia to receive a jug of wine. But, like Greg, Sylvia does not need anything Gary has. But, she does tell him she needs a new table built.

"With that request, Sylvia has just added to Gary's need for Sue's services."

Lownsbury walked back to the center of the dais, and placed the fingertips of each hand together.

"It is a problem. But, it is a problem with a fairly simple answer.

"Our little group discovers the need to develop a medium of exchange. This can be anything from beans, or trinkets to beads or baubles. Often times, throughout history, it has consisted of shiny stones and metals.

"Thus, our miner, Gwen, has agreed to trade her shiny, little stones to all of the Producers for their wares."

Turning around to face the Producers, Lownsbury gestured," Everyone, please reach inside the basket I gave you. Inside you will find a small bag of precious stones that we will use for our demonstration."

Turning to face the audience again, Lownsbury held a small copper disk between his thumb and finger.

"Today, we will be using a medium that we like to call pennies."

The familiar copper disc Lownsbury displayed between his fingers, glinted in the glow of the overhead lights. He paced again in front of the audience, still displaying the tiny one cent piece.

"This is the new medium of exchange our Producers have all agreed to use. Instead of trading product and service straight across, they can now exchange an agreed upon amount of pennies and each of them can purchase what they need from each other on their own terms and desires."

Lownsbury turned and pocketed the coin.

"Our little commune has just entered the realm of what has come to be known as Capitalism. Everyone, please notice that the definition of our economic dealings has not changed. Everybody still desires to be compensated for their product or service, we have just altered the medium of that exchange."

Lownsbury spread his hands.

"We have done something else too, ladies and gentlemen. Since we have moved from the physical bartering of goods and services to the trade of small, precious pieces of metal and stone, it becomes easier in the minds of our populace to offer meager scraps of coins to Doug."

Lownsbury turned to face the Producers.

"So listen carefully, everyone. Each time I ding this bell, I want each of the Producers to trade your coins back and forth to each other."

Lownsbury pointed to the shiny receptionist bell holding prominence on the small table.

"You will also find a schedule card in your baskets with which to guide you through the first round of trade, to get you started."

Lownsbury faced the audience, his eyes flashing.

"Each of our Producers will be trading their coins each time they hear that bell, for the demonstration of services rendered. Does everyone understand?

Nods of assent floated through the audience and those that occupied the dais.

"Very well."

(Ding)

Lownsbury reached over and rang the bell. The members of the group began exchanging coins back and forth as Lownsbury continued his speech.

"Our two Tokens, Phil and Tom, will not be engaging in this affair to any great degree at this point. But an occasional coin may be tossed their way by a friendly member. Our community has instead elected that our Tokens' room and board will be handled by the community, based on the overall need for the services that the two of them offer.

"Doug, of course will be given scraps only on the Producers' whim.

"But other issues will eventually arise, and our little tribe is about to make a fateful decision."

Lownsbury offered an ominous look to the audience and a sly smile spread wide across his face.

"They are about to elect me as their leader."

THREE

The Bowtie Principle

I was intrigued.

The unattainable epiphany that had floated just beyond my conscious reach had been growing stronger, yet remained just as elusive.

I was also beginning to realize the true ignorance of my colleagues; for I was learning a considerable amount from this professor. Lownsbury's method of instruction was as captivating as his soft, South African dialect of English.

I now had my recorder operational. I would have to transcribe the first part of the lecture from memory as soon as I was able. I also realized I needed to get permission from the professor in order to publish it, of course, but I was excited about that prospect. I decided I would make contact with Professor Lownsbury soon after the lecture.

The usher that I had seen running around, assisting Lownsbury, suddenly materialized at my side, startling me.

Tugging on my arm he said quietly, "Professor Lownsbury has asked that you join the group on the dais for the next part of the lecture, sir. If you don't mind."

I was a bit taken aback. "Me?" I asked.

The usher nodded emphatically, pulling on my coat sleeve, indicating that *"No"* would not be an acceptable response.

I found myself pulled along behind the odd little man to the dais. He showed me to a lone seat situated just behind Doug.

"What am I supposed to do?" I asked the usher with an air of disquiet. I had no idea what part I was destined to play in this lecture.

"Sit down right here," was all the odd man said as he turned and practically ran from the dais. He quickly vanished into the throng of people that had been stretching their legs as they awaited for the program to resume.

I looked to Doug for some answer as to what part I would play, but he was ignoring me. His attention diverted to the young lady that was seated behind him. I decided I would just wait and see what Lownsbury had in mind for me.

There was suddenly a tap on my shoulder. Surprised, I turned and found Professor Larimer Lownsbury standing behind me. Taken off guard by his sudden appearance, I clumsily stood, extending my hand. His handshake was as before, firm and abrupt.

With no preamble and barely a greeting, Lownsbury handed me a small, cheap wicker basket, and whispered quietly what he wanted me to do and precisely when to do it.

"Yes," I nodded, "I understand."

And then he was gone. His quick retreat nearly as startling as his appearance.

I took my seat again to await the role I would play in this lecture.

The lights in the hall flickered on and off as order was called again, and people quickly found their way to their seats, eager for the lecture to continue.

Professor Lownsbury suddenly appeared from the other side of the dais, and without a word, briskly strode to the small table and snapped the button on the brightly polished, desktop bell.

(Ding)

The chime resonated through the hall in perfect clarity. Everyone's attention was instantly captured and immediately, each of the volunteers began to exchange pennies with each other.

Another of the young ladies, seated down front, approached stage left and sat in one of six seats that were positioned behind Doug. Doug wandered over to the Producer's chairs, his basket held out in hopes of alms.

The professor smiled at the seamlessness of the exchange and brought his attention back to the audience.

"Our little group has a nice economy transpiring," he began, "Because of the medium of exchange that has been created, our members have become energized to provide the best products and services they can in hopes that more pennies can be charged. Even Doug has shown more fortitude in his begging efforts."

Doug smiled at the audience and raised his basket in mock solicitation.

Lownsbury strode easily over to Phil and placed a hand on his shoulder, "Our commune will visit Phil the Doctor for their injuries, and Phil the Teacher will teach their children daily on the history of their community and the other discoveries he makes during his day.

"Since the many roles of Phil is beholden to his group, he also teaches their moral convictions and laws."

As Lownsbury finished his sentence, he made his way easily to Tom's chair and referenced him similarly.

"Our Thief, Tom the Soldier protects our members from attacks of neighboring tribes. Stealing their enemies lives and occasionally conducting a raid to steal neighboring Producers' property when it serves the best interest of his community."

Lownsbury strode center stage.

"But another issue has arisen, ladies and gentlemen. Greg the Hunter has asked Sam the Engineer to design a log splitter.

"Sam wants five pennies for the job, but Greg is arguing that it didn't take her that long and will only pay her three.

"Now this is a simple matter that the two of them could likely sort out themselves. But Greg and Sam know each other. Have done business with each other for a long time.

"As our population grows, so does our unfamiliarity with each other. We strive to keep each other at arm's length. Our small towns where everyone knew each other and could talk with each other is dwindling. Replaced by large cities and sprawling metropolises in which we have little clue as to who we are dealing with, or what damage the other is capable of. With each new member of society, new laws are created; Micro-managed instructions as to how we should conduct ourselves. So many, in fact, that we become unsure of what the rules actually are."

Lownsbury was now at the *"Rules"* board, and making numerous, and seemingly random hash marks on the white surface.

"As our population grows so do our lawsuits and court proceedings. As well as the endless growth of rules to the point of absurd redundancy and an inability, and even an arbitrary unwillingness to enforce them."

He capped and pocketed his marker.

"Today, the internet has made it more and more possible to continue to create a chasm between us, relieving us of any social interaction. While, at once, the actual distance between us continues to shrink as we lay our heads on top of each other.

"We seek out that arms length ability to relieve ourselves of our responsibilities to each other. Our physical interactions with each other dwindle as does our empathy. We begin to put our faith into someone else to make our dealings with each other fair. And with that, we continue to elevate people to take the responsibility of fairness upon themselves. And often times, we will mistakenly pull these people from the Dregs."

Lownsbury pointed an accusatory finger at Doug. The young man feigned surprise and shrugged.

"These are the people we call the Rule-Makers, and our little society has just made the fateful decision to elect me as their Rule-Maker."

(Ding)

Lownsbury again rang the bell, and again, the volunteers on stage exchanged pennies with each other. Another young lady joined the other two in a seat behind Doug as Doug wandered over to the Producers, basket in hand.

"Please notice, ladies and gentlemen, that my newly acquired power is already such that each of them have a Pavlovian response to my bell."

Light sporadic laughter sounded through the hall again and Lownsbury smiled at his own witticism.

"As I take my throne let me explain the role of Rule-Maker.

"I will help settle Greg and Sue's dispute. And, I will settle the next one that occurs as well. Left alone, our little group would thrive fairly well. I could simply act as a mediator of disputes and let the commune carry on as they will. Just as our founders intended."

Lownsbury slowly turned his face to the audience. His voice lowered with his eyes as he smiled ominously.

"But, I won't," he said threateningly.

Laughter again filtered through the room as Lownsbury dropped his portentous act. His own good natured smile returning.

"I am now the Rule-Maker, and I get to set the most important rule of all. *There will be nobody higher in status than me.*"

The final commandment, I realized.

Lownsbury retrieved his marker and made another random hash mark in the field of the *"Rules"* board, and rotated the board on its wheeled based so that the audience could no longer see the front.

The back side of the board had a cloth draped over it and I wondered what form of revelation lay beneath it.

"A Rule-Maker is a Token. One side is the politician. He is the bureaucrat; the administrator.

"The other side of the Token is the Clergy. Both of these sides work in tandem with each other, or as rivals to *Control* the property of our Producer's.

"Politicians may typically realize better luck in the control of the tangible, and the clergy may find that the intangible property is easier to be had. But, both have the same desire to control our Producer's property. And, not just some of it. *All* of it.

"But that is a task that cannot be done all at once. It will take time.

Lownsbury strode center stage, his right hand extended, his fingers touching in that familiar gesture of articulation.

"Now, I want to be clear. This is not necessarily a conscious desire, and so it could honestly never be admitted to. But, it is an inevitable goal.

"The Clergy may say that his job is to provide aid and comfort to the poor and needy, to be a spiritual and moral guide. The Politician may claim his job is to keep the populace safe and ensure fairness to all. But, both will insist on the acquirement of an ever increasing amount of power to achieve these seemingly unattainable ends.

"And, that power translates as the ongoing acquisition of control over the property of the Producers. The Rule-Maker strives for control of both the tangible and intangible aspects of our people's property. Even their very lives.

"Neither of them can ever be satisfied with a fair share of their own. Their insatiable desire for complete control over each person's property is such that they will, time and again force their own people into desperate situations that will lead to, starvation, poverty, and eventually, once the people have had enough of them, bloody revolutions and war."

(Ding)

The chime resounded through the hall again, and everybody on the dais set about to their appointed tasks. Doug even managed to secure a couple of pennies this round, I noted.

Lownsbury paid scant attention to the proceedings occurring behind him. Confident they had transpired as need be.

"Let's not be confused," the professor continued, as everyone on the dais completed their appointed tasks and returned to their seats. "This does not necessarily mean the politician and clergy start their careers as evil people. Quite the contrary. Their original purpose is often thought of as noble. Desiring the betterment of their neighbors. Their families.

"Their roles are that which I refer to as the *MADD Syndrome,* which is defined this way: *Every cause, no matter how noble the issue that spawns its birth, will eventually cease to be about the cause and more so about the power and money that is wielded by the cause's upper echelon.*

There was a heavy pause as Lownsbury let that sink in.

"As our Rule-Maker's respective powers increase, so does their desire to maintain that power. And, to maintain that power means an ongoing effort to control the Producer's property. It has been said since the beginning of time that power corrupts. And, it does so without fail."

(Ding)

Lownsbury reached over and rang the bell again. The tiny chime wafted through the air of the auditorium with crystal clarity. Each volunteer dutifully exchanged their pennies with each other, and another young lady took a seat behind Doug.

"With my acceptance into the group as that tenth member, let me explain how we shall proceed. I will now introduce you to what I call my *Bowtie Principle.*"

I opened to a new page in my pamphlet program. The picture of a bowtie was prominent:

Bowtie Principle

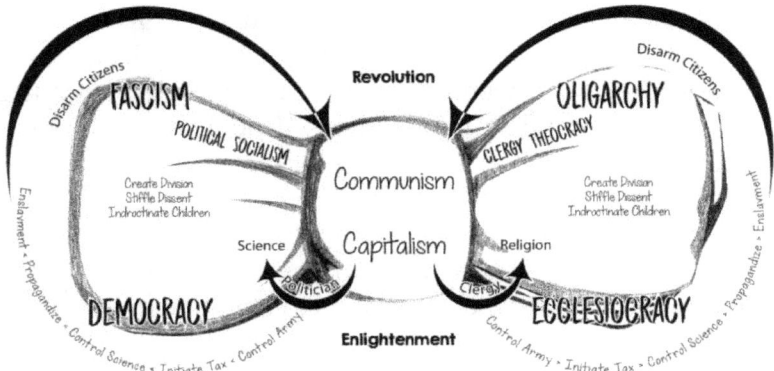

On the dais, Lownsbury pulled away the cloth covering the back side of the *"Rules"* board. A large graphic of the Bowtie lay beneath. A representation of what the pamphlet contained.

"Our group was formed in the center of this tie. They had a nice little community with capitalistic tendencies and institutions. The reason they are not completely communistic, is to be found in our earlier example of the dispute between Greg and Sue."

Lownsbury strode casually towards the Producers, and offered a casual gesture in their direction.

"Their argument begged the question: *'What is the definition of 'Fair'?'*"

A slight pause as he let the question hang in the air.

"Sam works with her mind. It is an intangible concept. Greg may not understand the years of learning and imagination that Sam has developed to justify what she charges for her time.

"Greg on the other hand, relies on hard physical labor, and the value of intangible property may elude him. He may have to work five hours to make the same wages that Sam is charging for just ten minutes of her time. This hardly seems fair to Greg."

Lownsbury resumed his gentle pacing, his soft, proper accent mesmerizing.

"Fairness is a difficult and very subjective concept, ladies and gentlemen. One that will never realize a consensual agreement. It is also the reason the Rule-Makers have a job. The guarantee of fairness has been a utopian promise made by

55

our Rule-Makers since our little group discovered that communism will eventually fail as the population grows.

"For instance, Producers will rarely, if ever, pay Doug to do nothing while each of them have to work hard for their pennies. Doug is a main beneficiary for entering capitalism. And, as we shall see, he is also the main catalyst for the groups progression towards socialistic oppression. And, Doug is prolific."

All of our eyes followed Lownsbury's as he stole a glance in Doug's direction. He now had five young ladies seated behind him. I began to understand the meaning behind their introduction.

Lownsbury resumed, "So in our Bowtie, our center is the working concept of our little community. It is the knot. The center on which everything else revolves.

"Our society is about to descend into the most common folly we, as humankind, plummet into every time they bring me, the Rule-Maker, into the fold. The folly that is committed is believing there is such a thing as a benevolent Rule-Maker."

Lownsbury smiled, then said, "The *Benevolent Folly Syndrome: There is no such thing as a benevolent government. No matter how badly we wish it to be true.*"

Lownsbury paused for only a second before continuing, "As the Rule-Maker, I have an insatiable thirst for control. And, worse still, since I am typically a Dreg, I will want to spread the traits of our Seven Deadly Sins for my own selfish advancement.

"To maintain the power over the Producers I have managed to procure, I will quickly come to see the value of Dregs as pawns in my schemes."

Lownsbury paused as if a thought occurred to him. He spread his hands.

"I feel compelled to point out an exception to this scenario. If a Rule-Maker is pulled from the Producers, as this country's founders originally intended - and if their character is strong enough - A Rule-Maker may be able to lead our group fairly well. But, this type of Ruler-Maker is very rare to find. It is also inevitable that this type of Rule-Maker will be demonized severely by the Dregs of that society."

Lownsbury searched the audience with a knowing smile, "But, I am a Rule-Maker that has been pulled from the Dregs. And, as a result, I am about to lead our group away from the neat bowtie knot of the little society in which they," Lownsbury pointed behind him to the Producers, "have created, into the outer fringes of the ties."

Lownsbury used his graphic to point out the aspects of the bowtie he had made. I followed along with the small representation in the pamphlet I held.

"As a politician, my desire is to head to the left side of the knot. Towards the utopian promise of socialism. If I am the clergy side of the coin, I have a desire to lead my society to the right side of the knot. Towards a theocratic utopia.

"As we enter the bowtie, our respective leaders will continuously propel us into the outer fringes of our bowtie. As our population grows, so does the speed in which we circle the periphery of the tie.

"Our Rule-Makers will do nothing to slow us down. As we circle the tie, their power increases and therefore there is no incentive for them to halt progress. They will circle the tie with ever increasing speed, often looking back to demonize many of their contemporaries who wish to slow the progression down to any degree. Epithets like "Right Wing" or "Left Wing" are simple slogans to describe someone who does not reside within the same area of the bowtie as themselves."

Lownsbury began his familiar stride easily moving back and forth across the dais, engaging every member of the audience.

"Let us study this further in terms of the history of the United States."

Lownsbury breathed deep, his eyes penetrating the crowd as they leaned forward, eager for his next words.

"At the time of the founding of the United States, the people of the country had just entered the center of the bowtie. It must be pointed out that even at the center of the tie, a society is never perfect" Lownsbury said with a sweep of his hand in gesture towards his volunteers. "It never is, nor will it ever be.

"But, it is as close to a fair society as you can hope for. And, it was at a point that the founders wanted it to remain stable for as long as possible. Not necessarily in stagnation, but within the realm of self governance.

"They wanted to ensure that we did not start drifting into the outer areas of the bowtie. We know this based in part on the language of the Constitution alone, but also in the plethora of writings our founders left behind."

The professor spread his arms.

"In order for their society to remain as free as possible, they knew they could not promote a theocratic form of government. Neither, could a free society shackle the clergy with rules and regulations."

Lownsbury lifted his eyebrows.

"Their solution was to simply prohibit the establishment of a religion based government.

"From the onset of this country's birth, the new United States was embroiled in a battle with Muslim pirates, and they could see, first hand, the destructiveness of a theocratic form of governance. They did not want to give the clergy the capability to wrest control of the people. But, they did not want them going without any say either.

"As with all Tokens, you need both sides of the coin to be complete. Our founders recognized the need for the clergy, as part of the Rule-Makers, to provide a moral compass for the politicians and a means to prevent us from heading up the left side of the bowtie; to keep us towards the middle of the bowtie as much as possible.

"They certainly did not want the United States to suffer through what had occurred with the Church of England, the corruption of the powerful Catholic Church, the revolution of Martin Luther or the onslaught of terror and slavery created at the hands of the Muslims.

"They agreed that they would not tell citizens how to worship but they would also not permit an established religion as part of the government."

Lownsbury paused, but only briefly.

"It has been argued, however, that our founders based our new government on Christian principles, and this is true. Of the three major branches of Judaism; which includes Christianity and Islam, Christianity may arguably allow for a secular form of government, much more easily than the other two.

"They realized though, that a country's government could not exist without politicians. But, they knew if they were pulled from the Dregs, the clergy would be hard pressed to keep them reigned in. So, the founders needed to put drastic, legal limitations on the politicians, to prevent damage to the society.

"So they set down a few simple pages of rules."

Lownsbury revealed the final third of the larger white board. On it were displayed six aged parchments.

The Constitution of the United States.

"To be clear, these rules were not directed towards our Producers," Lownsbury said, pointing to his volunteers. "No, These rules were made for me; the Rule-Maker. I was to be given very few, and very limited powers over the lives of these people behind me.

"But, consider, ladies and gentlemen, in less than three hundred years since the founding of the United States, our Rule-Makers have created thousands upon thousands of rules. Housed in massive libraries, each rule whittling, just a little at a time, the freedoms from its people."

Lownsbury strode purposefully back to the smaller board and, with the face of the *"Rules"* board still hidden from view behind the large Bowtie graphic, began making hash marks.

Randomly.

Hastily.

As if he were slashing at the board. His marker making squealing noises against the surface as he slammed the tip into it time and again.

"Each law that has been, and continues to be created, puts a restriction upon each of our liberties. Each law seeking to undermine the very fabric of those six sheets of paper. Thousands of rules that chip away at every little nuance of every word in every sentence that the framers wrote into our Bill of Rights, until today, those six pages are virtually meaningless.

"Each and every rule created, is designed with one purpose, and one purpose above all else: to give ever increasing power to me; the Rule-Maker.

"And, necessarily, every law that is made to benefit one person must necessarily harm someone else. So our Rule-Makers have made acres of other laws to attempt to portray the *image* of fairness."

Lownsbury's marker slammed again into the white board, his marks unseen but envisioned with audible clarity.

"Inevitably, the endless chaos of all these rules creates an unfair environment for everyone. And, as those acres of rules grow, it becomes unfair exponentially."

Lownsbury, his assault on the white board apparently ended, breathed an audible sigh. An uncomfortable silence lingered throughout the hall for a just a couple of seconds as Lownsbury finally put down his marker. He strode back to the center of the dais, and took another sip from his water glass.

"I think I just sprained my tongue," Lownsbury said with a slight smile. The audience smiled with him.

He took a final large gulp of water before setting the glass down, "Let us take another look at our Bowtie.

"If we were to follow the projected courses to fruition, the right side of the tie dictates that religion and a deity to be served is the meaning behind our spirituality. It is a Theocratic government that would be created.

"The left side dictates that Politics and Science would be adhered to and that our scientist, Phil, behind me, will eventually become our deity."

Phil smiled broadly as he adjusted his shirt tie. His gesture brought some mild laughter and a quiet relief from the intensity of the professors lecture.

"At the founding of the United States, our society was hovering at the bottom of the center of our bowtie. We call that the period of enlightenment," Lownsbury explained, pointing to the graphic.

"With the writing of our constitution, our founders sent us onto the path towards the left side of our bowtie. As I said, limiting the power of our politicians to make the travel as slow as possible.

"The founders wanted government to move at a snail's pace, with one exception. And, that was war and the protection of the country.

"The single responsibility all governments have for their nations is to keep it safe from foreign invasion. And, for our new country, the navy was the most important piece in keeping the nation safe."

He explained, "The immediate need to mobilize a navy resided in the fact that we had just been to war with a super power that possessed the largest navy in the world. The remnants of that war were still fresh in the collective memory, on both sides. The new United States also needed to trade with Europe, and they were plagued by Muslim pirates that relentlessly attacked any ship and coastal town within easy reach.

"The founders initially limited their control of an army, however. They did it purposefully with the intent of setting boundaries on me; the Rule-Maker. Allowing individual states the ability to control an army rather than federal politicians and its ever increasing bureaucracy.

"But, as we shall soon see, that was a very short lived concept."

Lownsbury cast his gaze in the direction of Tom the Soldier. He turned is eyes back to the audience a smile creeping across his face.

"I see a singular opportunity arise, ladies and gentlemen," he taunted, "My first act as Rule-Maker shall be to relieve our Producers from the responsibility of taking care of Tom."

That steady easy pacing.

"I shall take that duty upon myself. I will charge each Producer one penny every round, and I will offer Tom one penny as I keep five for myself. A mere pittance for the Producers to no longer have to worry about Tom's welfare.

"And, as we stated before, a repeating occurrence of **Benevolent Folly** on the Producer's part.

"This first step is very important, ladies and gentlemen. I will initially tell Tom that his job remains the same: To protect the community from his counterpart; the Villain. I have given him a wage; a paycheck. But the main thing I have done is..."

Someone in the audience shouted something I couldn't hear, But, again Lownsbury reiterated with his answer.

"That is correct," he acknowledged, pointing at the audience member, "It is the **Benefactor Syndrome.**

"It matters little that those six pages of rules, limiting my power, will also insist that Tom continue to protect the Producers. *I* am now Tom's benefactor, not them," he said, pointing to the Producer's. "Not any longer. Even though the Producer's are still paying the tab, it is filtered through me, and *I* am signing Tom's paycheck. Tom will now be beholden to me. Tom's main duty now is *my* protection. If I say, *'turn your weapons against the people, Tom'*, Tom will now do it.

"But, just as important, perhaps even more so, I have also enacted a tax on the Producers. This effectively takes control of a significant portion of the Producer's property.

"Remember, at the start of this demonstration, we determined that money was indeed our property. But, now that I have given myself the power to take it, I have effectively wrested control of a significant portion of the Producer's property under the guise of a seemingly benevolent reason; paying Tom. Which is what our group was doing anyway.

"But, I still cannot take control of everyone's property all at once. That would certainly start a revolution. If a revolution is to occur, I want to make sure Tom can easily outgun them. And, with those blasted pages of rules, I will have to do it just a little at a time."

From my position on the dais, I stole a glance across the hall. Everybody appeared just as enraptured by Lownsbury's lecture as I was. The deeper that Professor Lownsbury delved into his philosophies, the more animated and charismatic he became. Each perfectly pronounced syllable was another piece of a puzzle that seemed to snap perfectly into place.

"I have, nevertheless, increased my power immeasurably, and we have made big progress moving along our bowtie," he said pointing to his board.

"Because I have interjected myself into the economy of the community, I now have to bring an ally on board with me. I will pull him from the Dregs, of course, and I have named him *'The Economist.'* His job description is to create an ongoing image of fairness and prosperity to the people for my persistent meddling in their economy. But, this economist shall have an even more important role to be played as we shall see."

Lownsbury pointed to me and my pulse quickened.

It was time.

I stood with the basket that had been given to me and proceeded to the other side of the dais where the Producer's sat. They obviously were not privy to what my intentions were; their eyebrows lifting in question.

"To make things easier," Lownsbury said, his voice velvety smooth, "Each of the Producer's will now give my Economist all of their pennies in exchange for a packet of paper money. Paper money is lighter, easier to carry around, cheaper to make and, most importantly, suits my desires wonderfully."

Lownsbury's smile was wicked, his voice dripping with sarcasm, "And, I will generously, out of the goodness of my heart, give them all two pieces of paper for every piece of metal I confiscate."

My basket was filled with packets of dollar bills that had been cannibalized from a popular board game. As I had been instructed, I quickly began to pile the Producer's pennies into my basket, and in turn handed them each a pre-measured stack of the mock paper money.

(Ding)

Lownsbury had rang the bell again, and as instructed, each producer gave me back one of their pseudo-bills. I then walked over to Tom and handed him one, keeping the remaining five bills in my basket. I poured the pile of pennies from the basket into a container that had been set aside, as Lownsbury had instructed.

"As I mentioned, my thirst for control is endless," Lownsbury continued, "Our population has grown and with it, will be the need for technological advancements. Greg can no longer hunt enough meat or collect enough berries to feed everyone.

"With Sam's help, he has developed animal husbandry. He can plant corn and wheat and domesticate animals. He can now feed masses of people where only a few were fed before.

"But now, his livelihood is also far more dependent on the weather. One day he comes to me and says, *'We are in the middle of a drought. I cannot guarantee a solid harvest unless it starts to rain.'"*

(Ding)

The chime of the bell was sudden, and I found myself scurrying back to the Producers to, once again, relieve each of them of one of their paper bills. They were embroiled with exchanging their money back and forth with one another as well.

I then hurried over to Tom and handed him another bill, keeping another five in my basket.

Lownsbury turned and watched as one of the young ladies, assigned to a seat behind Doug, take her place. He grabbed his chin as if in thought, and held it in his hand.

"As I watch Doug the Sloth proliferate endlessly, an idea springs to my mind," Lownsbury said with a thoughtful look.

Lownsbury walked over to Phil and put a hand on his shoulder, "I decide to go to Phil the Scientist and I tell him, *'I will provide for you, Phil. Just like I do for Tom, if you do something for me. We need to take control of the Dregs, more specifically; the Sloth. They will soon outnumber all of us. I want you to proclaim to the group that we can make it rain if we simply appease the gods. And, to do that, we must offer sacrifice in the form of Doug's children.'"*

I saw Phil offer a genuinely startled look to the professor.

Lownsbury continued, "Well now, Phil says to me, *'How horrid, why must I do that?'*

"I say to Phil, *'I cannot present such an idea to the community. I can only enforce your findings. If your scientific discoveries indicate that such a sacrifice is needed, who among us could argue?'* I tell him, *'It will be best coming from you.'"*

Lownsbury's smile was wide as he pulled a separate wad of pseudo-money from his coat, and counting off a number of bills, placed a wad into Phil's palm, "Please take this small advance for your troubles."

He then walked over to Doug. With a single bill in hand, Lownsbury pressed it into Doug's palm and addressed the six young ladies, now seated behind him.

"Now ladies, each time I ring that bell, one of you will go back to your original seat while another takes your place. And, you will continue to rotate in this manner. Does everyone understand?"

Nods of assent could be seen.

Lownsbury smiled, "Very good." And, with a nod of approval, walked back to the small table.

(Ding)

I was now taking two bills from each Producer and offering one to each Phil and Tom, leaving now ten bills in my basket. My basket was quickly filling with the paper money.

"Now, ladies and gentlemen, we enter into what I term the **Sacrificial Syndrome.**

"Throughout all of mankind's history, the sacrifice of virgins has been a part of societal life. We typically view them as pretty young women, but with the exception of our volunteers here today," Lownsbury said with a sweep of his hand towards the ladies assembled behind Doug, "that is a very romanticized viewpoint. Virgin is simply an interpretation to mean children.

"These children are most typically pulled from the Dregs; children of the lowest classes within the populace. Doug, many times, is a willing participant, and many times, enthusiastically so because he will be paid for his sacrifice and be relieved of the burden of caring for another child. But, to offer the appearance of fairness, a top level Producer in line with this thinking can, and will at times, participate.

"As you can imagine, not every Producer is in agreement with this concept. Even today not everyone agrees with the process, but Phil, under my tutelage and support, has been successful in convincing most of the Producers of two very important things."

Lownsbury again became impassioned, emphasizing his next words with his hands.

"The first is that he, Phil, a simple man, has the ability to control nature," Lownsbury expressed with continued passion, "This is an extremely important concept, and as always, a tremendous point of contention, even to this very day.

"It is what I term as the *Rain Maker Syndrome: Since man first planted his food, the desire to control his natural environment, and the preyed upon naivety of the people by his leaders to think that he can, is unavoidable.*"

A brief silence enveloped the hall as people digested the meaning of this idea. To think that so many could fall prey to a timeless scam was halting.

Lownsbury resumed at the end of the perfectly timed pause, "The second thing that Phil has done, and this too is important, is to convince most of the Producers that the sacrifice of the children of the Dregs is a noble and worthwhile cause.

"Both of these concepts have existed in our collective since the beginning of time. Both are still as prevalent today as they were years ago, and both do one thing above all else."

Lownsbury cast his gaze expertly around the hall, smiling wickedly, "They give me; the Rule-Maker, an enormous amount of power."

(Ding)

I jumped at the sound of the chime, jolted with an awakening of how ancient these concepts actually were, and the true meaning behind them. I quickly went about my appointed duties.

"I now have unquestionable power over life and death of a significant amount of the population," Lownsbury said, "I am now charging an additional amount from everyone to make myself benefactor to an even greater percentage of the population. I have increasing power over the Producers by taking further control of their property.

"And, as I and all of us have just witnessed: I can actually control the very thoughts and beliefs of my Producers."

I was busy collecting money from the Producer's. They were also busy trying to pay me while continuing to exchange money between themselves.

I stole a glance in the direction of the Tokens and could see Phil and Tom eagerly awaiting their pay. The demonstration was becoming a bit intense.

"I have learned that a word from Phil is treated as gospel," Lownsbury crowed, "He becomes a scapegoat if I need him, but as long as Phil tells the Producers what I want them to hear, I can increase my power exponentially.

"So I now decide. I need as much control of Phil as possible. I take control of Phil the Teacher, in the same way I did Phil the Scientist. And, with his whole hearted acceptance in receiving a raise, I now have the power over the education of the Producer's children!"

The professor's eyes flashed in excitement, his enthusiasm catching.

"Since I am signing Teacher Phil's paychecks, and giving him a raise, he will now teach the Producer's children what I want them to learn," Lownsbury proclaimed with acute confidence.

"The Producers are happy for they do not have to worry about Phil anymore, their children are still being taught history, at least for now. And, there is no reason to doubt my motivations, our Producers are deep and they are falling deeper into the *Benevolent Folly Syndrome*."

Lownsbury's smile was wide, his eyes even deeper and more penetrating.

"I have, by now, taken even further control of the Producers minds. Their thoughts. Their beliefs. And, I am so bold as to even be charging them for it," he laughed.

"It has taken years, but it is working beautifully." Lownsbury was rubbing his hands together, smiling in glee. His acting was a superb compliment to the demonstration.

(Ding)

The bell was struck again. The intensity of the demonstration was growing. I was now collecting three bills from each Producer and handing Phil two bills, Tom one, and keeping fifteen for Lownsbury.

I could hear the Producer's grumbling to each other about the amount of money that was going into my basket. They were becoming visibly annoyed.

How interesting, I thought.

"But, I am not yet finished," Lownsbury boasted.

"I am originally a Dreg which means my greed is growing exponentially with my power, and it is contagious.

"Not satisfied that the Clergy side of my Token has a singular monopoly with charity for the Dregs. I again go to the Producers and say, *'Look at poor Doug the Sloth over here. How about I charge you just a wee bit more, and I will take care of him, as well?'*"

Lownsbury straightened, and with a sneer, his voice filled with contempt, said, "This time I don't even wait for a response from them."

(Ding)

The Producers were now really grumbling about the four bills they each had to pay me as I now included Doug into the mix of receivers. The chaos of the money changing was growing.

"I now am charging four bills from each of the Producers," Lownsbury summarized, "I have given raises to my two tokens, Phil and Tom. And, I have included Doug as a recipient by giving him a paycheck. I now have total control over all three Tokens as well as all of the Producers."

Lownsbury's basket was indeed piled full of the fake money. I was having a bit of a time keeping up with the changing rules.

"I hear the Producers starting to grumble," Lownsbury said, "Some of them are starting to question all the propaganda and the pseudo-science I am having Phil espouse. Some don't like the fact that they are financing Doug and wish to see some production from him. Some also don't like financing the human sacrifices that are occurring over in Doug's corner of the world.

"Some are beginning to realize that their children do not have an accurate understanding of their own history, but they are seeing that Phil is making an increasing amount of money every time he makes a claim that he can make it rain.

"In other words, ladies and gentlemen, my Producer's are beginning to realize all the power I am amassing and they are becoming wise to what is happening."

(Ding)

I was thinking quick now as I tried to wrap my head around the money that needed to change hands. I noticed that some of the Producer's were no longer trading with each other as they attempted to satisfy their requirements to my basket.

"My first response to combat the dissatisfaction occurring among the Producer's," Lownsbury continued, "is to instruct Phil the Teacher to indoctrinate the children into demonizing my dissenters. Phil will now instruct the youth to castigate and ridicule those that deny my propaganda. Including their own family!"

Lownsbury raised a hand in a gesture to the children still picketing outside the lecture hall doors.

"Phil is now working double time to remove all critical thinking from the youth by no longer teaching their country's history and is now teaching *my* version of history and only the pseudo-science that keeps him employed by *me*.

"And, every day I am able to see my power grow."

Lownsbury rubbed his hands together in front of an iniquitous smile.

"There is no way I will relinquish my power now. They will have to drag my dead, mutilated body out of the Rule-Makers Mansion. And, with Tom to protect me, it will cost the Producers dearly to try it."

Lownsbury walked about the stage, pointing at his Tokens, "Phil and Tom both know which side their bread is buttered, they will not sway or falter.

"Phil is becoming increasingly successful in teaching the Producer's children to stand up, violently if need be, to stifle any criticism of my propaganda."

Lownsbury walked over to Phil and, from his own stash of bills, counted off a few more to Phil. He then walked back over to the table.

(Ding)

I was now grabbing handfuls of bills from the Producer's to deliver to Phil, Tom and Doug as the girls behind Doug played musical chairs.

Lownsbury retrieved several large pieces of cardboard from behind the larger white board and began placing them between the chairs of the Producers. He explained his actions, his excitement growing as he spoke.

"As dissent continues to grow among the Producers I need to effectively create divides among them. To weaken them and prevent their dissent from spreading.

"Those damned six sheets of paper," he said with disdain, pointing at the aged parchment still displayed on the white board, "Say that I can't outlaw their congregating, but I can discourage and manipulate it. I will separate out the populace by race, by economics. I will place barriers to promote misguided beliefs and to keep them from congregating. I will effectively distract them by keeping them fighting amongst themselves.

"I will promote conflict among them to keep them from talking about anything substantive. They will instead talk endlessly about their victimhood, their perceived oppression from others, and they will fall prey to their ever increasing envy of which I will perpetuate."

Lownsbury was becoming more animated and his growing excitement was contagious. Everyone was on the edge of their seats.

"I will sow the seeds of discontent by allowing the seven terrible sins of destruction free reign in the society. I will sanctify lust, greed, gluttony. I will encourage wrath and sloth. And most of all, I will inspire envy.

"I will further spread deceit by attempting to convince the Producers that if it weren't for those six pages of rules tying my hands, we could have peace and tranquility."

Lownsbury, advancing on the Constitution, smacked it disdainfully with the back of his hand.

"These simple, outdated pages of rules are all that stand in the way between them and a free loving, communistic utopia that they once enjoyed," Lownsbury breathed contemptuously, pointing to the aged looking parchments behind him.

"And as *Benevolent Folly* continues to ensnare them, and a new generation comes into the society with no history as to how peaceful life was before I came to so much power. And, with the teaching of my approved propaganda, many will actually come to believe it."

Lownsbury peeled off a few more paper bills, and again shoved them into Phil's palm.

"I have taken control of most of the Philosophers, which include Phil the Scientist, Phil the Teacher, and now I also control Phil the Press and Phil the Entertainer. Spreading my deceit through the written word, their evening entertainment, and their daily instruction.

"I have successfully interjected myself into every part of the Producer's everyday lives. The people's every belief will be through my dictate. Their every waking thought will now center around me."

Lownsbury's eyes were alive as he paced back and forth across the dais.

"People will be unable to take a bite of food without first paying homage to *me*."

(Ding)

Lownsbury held a pause with perfect timing.

"I will create further divides by taking individual Producers to the side and make deals with them. I will play upon their greed and offer them their fellow man's money for favors in return."

I had been anticipating this part of the demonstration and I hoped I would be able to pull off the instructions I had been given.

"With Gary, I will offer to buy his products at a substantial markup to ensure that my strong arm, Tom, has the finest in weaponry and can easily outgun everyone that may stand in my way."

(Ding)

As I collected an enormous amount of bills from the producers, I also handed Gary a large bundle of previously collected bills back to him. He smiled greedily at the offered money. I thought how interesting that his reaction was instinctually the same as if the money had been real. Certainly, Lownsbury was correct. Greed was such an easy sin to proliferate.

I heard Lownsbury behind me still offering his insights. He was now proceeding with a level of haste.

"I will offer Greg money to produce the quantity and the kind of food I want him to. With his cooperation, we will keep food prices high and together we will make a fortune."

(Ding)

I was moving fast now. Collecting bills but now handing both Gary and Greg another bundle of bills back to them.

"I will force Gwen to give me all of her precious stones. I remind her how useless they are now that I have already replaced the Producer's pennies with paper money. Money that I have created myself. Paper that is no longer the legal property of the Producers; it is currency that I can make worthless at any time."

How deeply interesting, I thought. The look of greed on these people's faces was increasing with each small bundle I handed out, regardless of Lownsbury's last statement of its worthlessness.

I suddenly realized I no longer had the ability to run over to Tom, Phil and Doug. But, realizing that themselves, the three of them had come over to surround the Producers and me.

The chaos of paper shuffling had become enormous. I was busy acting as money changer for everyone. Counting each person their amount of money and depositing increasing amounts back into Lownsbury's basket.

"I will offer Sam and Sue huge government contracts for creating bunkers for me and my family, to protect us from the inevitable wrath of the Producers."

(Ding)

The money changing was chaotic. The wad of bills I was handing out was still unequal to the amount I was receiving, and most of the producers had practically given up exchanging anything amongst themselves.

"I will continue my indulgence by telling Sylvia that it isn't fair that Gary and Greg are making so much more money than her, and I will now charge them double taxes to make up for her share. In fact, I will give her an additional stipend for doing nothing at all. An offer she greedily accepts."

(Ding)

"Doug is a mindless, but extremely important pawn in my schemes. He will be a great shield if Tom needs it, and a disposable commodity for myself when the time comes. I will chastise everybody for not doing enough to help poor Doug. And, I will hit them now with the onset of *The Charity Scam Syndrome.*"

(Ding)

The producers were becoming increasingly panicked as I struggled to keep up. Their anger was actually feeling very real and increasing each turn.

Lownsbury described it perfectly.

"Everyone is full of envy and greed as they watch their neighbors make deals with me. Their covetous hands grasp for a sliver of the pie that *I* fully control, no longer able, or willing to trade amongst themselves. It is now *my* money they covet, *my* goodwill they lust for, *my* favor they desire."

Lownsbury's voice was raised. The audience was captivated at the drama unfolding before them.

"And, as I look upon the wasteland that their world is becoming, I take final control over the life and death of everyone on this dais. In one sweeping grab of ultimate power, I take over control of the biggest token Philosopher of them all; **Phil the Doctor**.

"All of The Philosophers are now completely beholden to me!" Lownsbury practically screamed in delight, his arms raised high above his head.

(Ding)

There were a few audible gasps as the impact of this statement was realized.

"And, eventually as delightful, emotion driven sin corrupts everyone in its seven tentacled embrace, their anger will peak and wrath will conquer their very souls.

"It is now my own self-preservation that reigns and I offer up a scapegoat upon which they may unleash their anger!"

I suddenly felt Lownsbury grab my arm, throwing it high into the air in front of him. His paper money spilling out of my hands to cover the floor.

"Behold! He that has taken your lives, your property, your souls, now stands before you! It is he that must be cast out, and we must never again allow another like him to survive!"

I was caught off guard. I was actually horrified. Everyone looked as if they were about to lynch me for real, so impassioned Lownsbury had made the crowd.

Lownsbury continued his lecture as I stopped what I was doing and stared wide eyed at the Producers. Hoping they would not leap from their chairs and tie me to a rail.

"The time has come ladies and gentlemen, to round up all of the money changers and the greedy bankers and the economists. Sadly, they and their families will need to be put to death. It is unfortunate, but I stand at your side to see us through this difficult time. I stand with the people. Together we will be strong. Together we can do it."

Lownsbury walked over to the white board. His fist, clutching his chest in mock remorse, yet his face displaying a pain that felt all too real.

"The founders could never have envisioned what this future was to become," Lownsbury continued, still speaking as if he were a politician, "We must live in today. And so, it is with a heavy heart, my fellow producers, for the benefit of everyone, that I finally be unshackled from these six, outdated pieces of paper."

In one movement of his hand, Lownsbury tore the parchments from the board and let them fall in a crumpled heap to the floor.

He lingered a pause in his usual style of perfect timing before he resumed normally, "I shall have some dissenters, of course. Producers that somehow know their history and can see right through my subterfuge. But, they will be few and far between. And, if the Producers get wise and start tearing down the blockades that I have placed between them. If they begin to talk amongst themselves, and listen to my critics of which I have been unsuccessful in taking control. If their dissent continues to grow even after they have taken out the scapegoat I have offered. And, if their anger looks as if it will soon be rightfully turned towards me, I have one *Final* response."

Lownsbury walked back over to his volunteers and grabbed Tom's arm.

"Tom shall now enforce my Final Law. No longer will any form of firearm be allowed among the populace. Those caught with a firearm defending themselves will join the Economist in the gallows."

Lownsbury let Tom's arm drop. He then walked in front of the Producer's, pointing to them in turn.

"Gwen works for me, Sylvia works for me. Sue and Sam are paid by my unions, and now - Gary. Gary as the manufacturer of weapons, works exclusively for me now."

Lownsbury made his way to the *"Rules"* board and scratched the final hash mark on the board. In one flourishing move he turned it around for us to see.

The hash marks were arranged in such a way as to spell out the word, "**SOCIALISM**"

The crowd was eerily silent. I could hear one woman weeping. Everyone could see and feel the full impact of what had been transpiring in this country and how it had manifested itself. More importantly, they realized the future that awaited it.

Everyone on the dais returned to seats, the floor was littered with paper money, everything was in disarray.

Lownsbury his head high and calm, strode easily to the center of the dais. His soft South African inflection even more soothingly pronounced.

"Over the years we have moved at an ever increasing pace around the edges of our bowtie ladies and gentlemen. Moving dangerously close to a fascist society. The United States does appear destined to get there, with an inevitable outcome to follow," he said indicating the top word of the bowtie.

As I looked to the graphic, the single word *Genocide* bounced from the page. A murmuring shiver ran through the crowd.

"Every Socialistic society will eventually lead to some form of genocide," Lownsbury said softly, pointing to Doug. "Every time a dictator leads his people toward genocide, the idea is made palatable for the public at large. Keep in mind, this is not done with one hundred percent approval, nothing ever is. But, the terms and conditions are managed so that the populace at large will not, nor are they allowed to disapprove.

"Consider that less than twenty percent of the German population believed in the Nazi cause, or even followed the Nazi path. But, it mattered little. The German Producers were starving. They were defeated. A Rule-Maker, with the strength of Hitler, following this blueprint we have outlined here today, was ripe to take over.

"People are so busy as Producers, making a living for themselves and their children, that they are as frogs in a pot of water set for slow boil. Their initial misguided belief in benevolence of government will each and every time, lead to this inevitable end.

"By the time they notice what I, as the Rule-Maker, am really up to, it is too late to accomplish much peacefully. As with every socialistic culture, eventually we will begin killing each other. Just as we did during our revolution, during our first civil war, so it will be for our next.

"And, all because of me.

"*The Rule-Maker*."

Lownsbury said this final sentence as if he had seen this scenario play out a hundred times before. I could literally see the exhaustion in his eyes.

I suddenly realized that the usher had moved the wired microphone from the stage to a small podium set up in the center aisle. There was undoubtedly a question and answer phase set to occur, but I was sincerely praying that Lownsbury would call a bathroom break before he started. I was very grateful when my prayers were answered.

Four

Question and Answer

I had found my original seat in the audience and was anxious to see how the question and answer session would go. Although I had witnessed many in the audience that were of a single mind with the professor, there were bound to be dissenters and given the professors intellect, that form of drama was always entertaining.

Plus, after two hours of hearing Lownsbury talk, I was anxious for another voice.

A long line was forming behind the arranged podium, it reminded me of standing in line for a music event. Early arrivals would be first served and each were jockeying for the closest position.

I was flipping through the short program that had been handed out when Lownsbury's *Syndromes of Civilization* page caught my eye:

Syndromes of Civilization.

Rain Maker Syndrome: *Since man first planted his food, the desire to control his natural environment and the preyed upon naivety of the people by his leaders to think that he can.*

Egg Syndrome: *Every scientist's findings should be viewed with a jaundiced eye, especially if the scientist is financed by government, for the findings will change tomorrow and the next.*

Benevolent Folly Syndrome: *There is no such thing as a benevolent government.*

Charity Scam Syndrome: *Charity done by the clergy may be a noble endeavor, but when attempted by the Politician presents as nothing more than a scam.*

Benefactor Principle: *Each of us are beholden to that person who signs our paycheck.*

Sum Total Syndrome: *Sum total of the Egg Syndrome, the Benevolent Folly Syndrome, Charity Scam Syndrome, and Benefactor Principle. - The motivations of anyone paid by government should never be trusted.*

Sacrificial Syndrome: *Removal of the undesired young, especially among the dregs of society. And, the desire to create a means to perform this function that is palatable to the public at large.*

'I Can't Believe You're Not Me' Syndrome: *The inability to accept that your ideas and beliefs may not be shared by everyone. Part of the envy side of the sins, and one that is very prolific in politics and religion.*

Morality Syndrome: *Women control the morality of a society and direct the Male population as to the ethics and principles to be followed.*

MADD Syndrome: *Every cause, no matter how noble the issue at its start, will eventually cease to be about the cause and more so about the power and money that is wielded by its upper echelon.*

Selfish Paradox: *The act of being so selfish, that you don't have the time or the inclination to truly be selfish.*

Slavery Syndrome: *Mankind will always allow and nurture and defend the institution of slavery.*

Lobster Syndrome: *That state of being in which the enjoyment of your meal is overshadowed by the amount of work it takes in consuming it.*

US Government Syndrome: *Anytime the government goes to war with a portion of the public, it is for the takeover of the perceived infraction, not the ending of it.*

Barbarian Syndrome: *There will always be barbarians of the world that will threaten every civilization. The only answer to barbarian plagues is their complete destruction. The minute they are acquiesced to by refusing to commence that destruction, is the minute that starts the decline of that civilization. (Start the Suicide Syndrome)*

Suicide Syndrome*: Every organism from large to small, from an individual to a civilization, will eventually tire of its existence and take steps to end it.*

Scientific Syndrome: *Scientists will vilify the advancement of competing scientific theory to stifle any rivalry for research money.*

The lights began to blink on and off, terminating intermission, and it was only a few seconds before Professor Larimer Lownsbury strode back to center stage.

"Ladies and gentlemen, I do appreciate your attendance here today. It was a beneficial endeavor for me, I hope it was for you as well. I presume you have many questions, so without further delay, lets proceed to our question and answers. As a bonus, I have invited a number of our protestors to join us in today's question and answer session to grace us with their wisdom of the ages."

Laughter rocked the hall, causing Doctor Lownsbury to pause with a broad smile.

He quickly resumed, "We handpicked our protestors based on their ability to articulate their thoughts, hopefully without the espousing of their mindless banalities.

"Young lady," Lownsbury said, pointing to the first member in line, "What can I do for you?"

"Thank you, Doctor Lownsbury," the woman stated with a coy smile, "I truly enjoyed the lecture. I heard you mention the Charity Scam Syndrome, what is that specifically?"

Lownsbury gave a slight nod, "As I mentioned earlier, Politicians and Clergy are two sides of the same coin. They are not interchangeable and it takes both sides to check each other to successfully lead a nation.

"The clergy may often be envious of the ability for politicians to tax people, and a politician can envision the potential of enormous power in providing some perceived charity to the public. Neither are equipped to handle the others proclivity well, but they each will try it, given an opportunity.

"The actual *Charity Scam Syndrome* works like this: The politician will create a problem. He then offers a pseudo-solution with a charity that can be donated to. It is a pseudo-solution in that it will never solve the problem, but offers a feel good solution that can perpetuate the problem with the politician involved as the owner or interested party of the charity. Typically the politician and his comrades involved with the charity become wealthy. However, the problem escalates and the greed of the politician entices him to initiate a mandatory tax for the perceived, perpetual problem, while steadfastly never solving it."

Lownsbury sighed quietly, "Let me offer an example of this idea.

"One of the larger issues of today, around the country, is that politicians are inviting the career homeless to their towns. And, as we will remember, a politicians goal is the perpetuation of the Dregs.

"When the public outcry becomes too loud to ignore, because their towns are becoming trashed with hundreds and thousands of these Dregs, the politician declares their hands are tied by some imaginary force and actually blame the public for giving the Dregs money.

"So, the politician offers a solution. A pseudo-solution. Instead of donating to the bums personally, give me..." Lownsbury laughed at his intentional *faux-pas*, "...I, of course mean this charity over here, your money, and they will take care of the bums for you."

Lownsbury smiled, "Notice, ladies and gentlemen, that the problem remains. The panhandlers still wander the streets of the taxpayers' towns. The politicians will not ship them out, they are a golden goose.

"They, instead will feed them and invite more of them and collect increasing money through the charity. The problem perpetuates until the emergency services; such as the police and fire, become so over-burdened that the charity, one day, becomes mandated as a tax.

"But, the homeless have now become a permanent fixture. The problem is never solved. This is a supreme example of the politician perpetuating the Dregs for his own power."

Lownsbury touched his fingers together.

"Let me clarify: I speak here now of career homeless. Not the legitimate few that fell onto hard times. Bums are career homeless; purposely avoiding any attempt to become a Producer, and caring little for the hands that are feeding them. If they truly were thankful for the handouts that the Producers offer them, they would not trash their towns.

"Legitimate homeless; those that have fallen on hard times; are striving to get back into the camp with the Producers; to make something of themselves, are not those that stagnate within the Dregs and the sins of sloth.

"Thank you, Miss. Next question, please."

Another young lady that had been part of the demonstration, (I had seen her sitting behind Doug at one point) approached the microphone.

"Hi Doctor Lownsbury, I was wondering. You said that communes are unrealistic and don't work. But, I personally think that that form of selfless living is great and we should all be a part of one. It promotes free love and brotherhood."

Lownsbury held up his hand, stifling any rambling that appeared to be in the making, "Actually, it does no such thing. It is not selfless living, it is Selfish Paradox."

The girl's dreamy, far-away look conveyed a complete lack of understanding of what Professor Lownsbury had just said.

He elaborated, "A selfish paradox is defined as somebody that is so selfish he or she doesn't have the time to be selfish. For instance. We have all come across people in our lives that given a choice between sitting on the couch and watching TV, or helping his buddy move a piece of furniture into their home, will choose the couch.

"Unfortunately, helping the buddy would have been the actual selfish thing to do. By helping the buddy, he could better persuade that buddy to reciprocate when his own need arose.

"This manifests as believing that anything you feel like doing, at any given time, should be accepted and even embraced, regardless of what anybody thinks or believes about it. That is unrealistic and the epitome of selfish paradox.

"Notice also that you said what *You* think everybody should do. That too, is a Syndrome of Civilization. It is the *I Can't Believe You're Not Me Syndrome.*

"Communes are, and should be, voluntary. If you desire to live in a commune of your choosing, more power to you. But, it is immoral to attempt to dictate, through armed government force, that everyone else must follow in *your* self-righteous footsteps.

"People who are deep into this syndrome, aren't content with living their own lives to their own desires, they must also bend others to their will. Forcing others to live according to their dictates, they will never be happy minding their own business, or tending to their own affairs. They must also infiltrate their opinions into other people's lives.

"Everyone has this syndrome to some degree, but it is the people like you, miss, that insist that everyone else must follow *your* path.

"You might consider that a better mantra for your professed hippy lifestyle would be, *'live and let live'*."

"Well, isn't it just as immoral," the young lady labored, "to force me to conform to your societal ideal?"

Lownsbury raised his eyebrow at the question, "Yes it is. Hence the term *voluntary*. You should be able to live your life as you choose. However, by relegating yourself to the societal Dreg, you should not have any say as to the conduct of the society at large. Be a Dreg if you like. That should be your freedom and right. But, your choice as arbiter of societal decay should not be rewarded."

Lownsbury scratched his forehead, his brow wrinkled, "When I think of communes, I am reminded of every movie in which the shallow are enlightened, by shedding their worldly possessions to live in a commune that they have stumbled upon, only to achieve ultimate enlightenment at the end of the movie by the discovery of Capitalism."

Lownsbury smiled at this final remark and pointed to a young man standing his turn behind the girl, effectively dismissing her.

A young man approached the podium. He was rather slovenly dressed. I had not seen him during the program and concluded he must be part of the protestors. When he spoke, he proved rather articulate, although long winded.

"Yes, professor, I have heard you say how diversity is dangerous and leads to bloodshed. But, our society would disagree with you, and in fact most believe that it makes us stronger as a people. Wouldn't you agree that diversity of thought and diversity of people promote cultural enhancement? We all learn from different cultures and different races, wouldn't that be considered a good thing?"

There was sporadic applause throughout the auditorium as the young man's expression was welcomed by those with similar viewpoints.

Lownsbury waited until quiet again surrounded the hall, then answered succinctly with one word.

"No."

Laughter erupted throughout the hall at the simplicity of the answer and its dichotomy to such a long and meandering question.

The boy stood there stunned. It was obviously not the answer he had expected. Lownsbury smiling, explained.

"I have often said that diversity is deadly. This is what I mean by that.

"Let's imagine that there are two different farms. Separated by several miles.

"One family is Dutch, the other is Irish. Both families consist of extended generations from grandparents to the newborns. Both enjoy their respective language, traditions, cuisine, and etiquettes.

"Separated, these families enjoy visiting, and trading. Perhaps they even enjoy the occasional Romeo and Juliet marriage that introduces new ideas, or traditions to each family. But they keep to their respective farms. Their own territory.

"This can be defined as good, healthy diversity. An exchange of theories and opinions that are not forced upon each other, but can be regarded, or even discarded, as respective evaluations dictate.

"The negative side of diversity begins when one family's home burns to the ground and, with no place left to go, that whole family moves into their neighbors home.

"Unquestionably, the guest family will huddle. They will not assimilate because there are just too many of them to do that effectively. The guest family will begin to feel entitled. They will naturally want to maintain their own traditions, their own cuisine and habits.

"The host home will, naturally, feel invaded. Put upon. Taken advantage of. The divisions of thought, traditions, culture will undoubtedly breed distrust, suspicion and finally, hatred.

"Over time, and through several generations, assimilation may occur, and a whole new culture may arise.

"But, if the host family is too overwhelmed, the natural instinct for survival says to fight and kill; on both sides. And, eventually neighbors, that were once friends, become bitter enemies.

"Remember, diversity is the antithesis of unity.

"Next question."

The boy left with a look of dissatisfaction on his face. As if he had somehow lost a battle, but did not yet realize that the war was also over.

The usher was there to ensure that the boy did not dawdle with an attempted verbal parry, guiding him away to let the next person to the microphone.

A well dressed older man, perhaps in his fifties, put his mouth too close to the microphone. His question was loud and a bit muffled through the screeching of the speakers, and he had to pull back and ask his question again.

"Doctor Lownsbury, you said that your counterparts in the category of Philosophers should not receive awards, or graven images, and all that. I was wondering, does that include you?"

His question prompted random laughter, and Lownsbury even smiled at the soft dig.

"I doubt if my peers will ever reward me with a statue. I do not share their narrow-minded, political group think. I forthrightly criticize their intellect. I openly explain how oppressive and genocidal their ideas and beliefs are. I do not join their chorus of political correctness. And, as a result, we share a mutual level of dispassion in the giving and receiving of any of *their* treasured accolades."

Lownsbury smiled, "Thank you, good question, next please."

"Thank you Professor," an older man said. He was balding, short and wore glasses, He appeared to be part of the group of protestors.

How foolish, I thought, for an older man to be joining in the chorus of the ignorant youth and I wondered what lunacy he would utter.

I didn't have to wait long.

"I was wondering how you rectify science and religion in your theories. professor? One pathway, that of science, is to the truth, and the other is outdated superstitions and speculation?

You seem to hold both in the same regard and on equal footing, and I can't understand how any self-proclaimed, learned man could openly embrace that point of view."

Lownsbury looked silently at the man for several, long seconds. Something seemed to catch his eye and I saw him stoop down and pick up a piece of paper laying near his feet. It was a fragment of the rumpled Constitution that he had ripped from the board at the tail end of the lecture, and that was now laying in a misshapen heap on the floor next to him. He took his time opening the paper, folding the flaps carefully back. Regarding the writing as he smoothed the wrinkles between his hands.

The hall had gone silent; eerily silent. A random cough was heard but was quickly stifled.

Lownsbury looked up slowly.

"Sir, you are a fool."

The hall suddenly erupted in applause. Lownsbury was drowned out for several long seconds as the thunder reverberated, eventually fading enough for him to continue.

"It is utterly reckless for us to simply dismiss the ideas and beliefs of our ancestors. These were people that could challenge many an intellect in modern society. You, and the ignorant like you, so arrogantly assume that we have new ideas and concepts. Horse shit!"

The crowd again erupted, but the deafening applause died quickly.

"To say our so called *'new ideas'* are more correct than thousands of years of observations of our natural world; to say that our ancestors were archaic or misguided; that they had no understanding as to the workings of the human mind and instincts, is the most audacious, conceited presumption any mature individual could think to utter.

"Ancient writings of learned civilizations have long stood the test of time. They have launched hundreds of civilizations into a search for something far larger and more meaningful than themselves, only to be returned to time and again for the wisdom they bestow."

Lownsbury pointed an accusatory finger.

"You labor under a simple-minded misconception, sir. You mistake science as the only bearer of truth when both science, and religion are defined as a search for legitimacy; a speculation in search of an answer. What we commonly mistake for truth is merely whatever our leaders tell us it is at any given time. Usually under an umbrella of political expediency.

"Religion will tell you that something spectacular occurred. Perhaps nothing more than an epiphany. Science merely seeks to explain *how* that something occurred.

"Religion explains the time tested rules of how a people can form a society in order to live together, and the spiritual tenets that help create a fulfilling life.

"Science does not dictate morality in which a society is to live with each other, it is meant to give natural meaning to supernatural concepts; to explain the unexplainable. But, again, both are mere speculation.

"Science and religion do not have to be diametrically opposed. Science and religion are often able to work in tandem with each other. It is only the propaganda vomited by our leaders; both the politicians and clergy, that dictate whether that will take place or not. Religion does not seek to discredit science, nor does science reciprocate. It is only man's ambitions and desires that mandate opposition; typically in the quest for power over the people. A timeless lesson as we have learned here today.

"Some religious leaders will decry science in that it seeks to destroy God, while some scientists childishly claim that the destruction of God is their intent. But, neither are true. It is only man's quest for power that seeks to warp science and religion's true intent. It is the Rule-Maker's efforts that will cause the uneducated populace to swing wildly back and forth as they blindly follow those nefarious leaders."

Lownsbury shook his head with a level of unconcealed disdain.

"To live a full life, man must not discard his spirituality any more than he should discard his reason. A concept that only the wisest among us seem to posses."

Lownsbury's voice was brimming with passion, "Ideas like the ability to self govern, or to do unto each other as you would have done to you; these are timeless concepts. Only the ignorant; the imbecile, would sanctimoniously discard these writings as outdated, believing their own narrow minded perception to be the only truth."

He now held the crumpled parchment in front of him in emphasis, "It is the wise man that understands the need to embrace these two concepts."

Lownsbury shook his head, "No sir, it is not me that must rectify my theories of science and religion, I believe that would be you."

This time it took nearly a full minute for the applause to dwindle. People were on their feet their arms held high above them as they brought their hands together in excitement. It was perhaps the most raucous ovation I had ever heard a speaker receive. Even I was caught up in the laudation.

I saw the man who had asked the question storm from the auditorium in a huff. Behind him, two others fell out of line and followed him through the doors. Perhaps a bit humbled by the tongue thrashing the last question asker had received. I could imagine the propaganda that the dimwits would undoubtedly espouse to their brethren outside. Further confirming in their minds the embracing of misinformation concerning Lownsbury and his teachings.

The applause finally began to dwindle as people returned to their seats. Lownsbury remained silent for a long, several seconds as order was again instilled.

Then he smiled and mumbled under his breath, "Dumbass."

Laughter cascaded through the room like shattered glass, chiming delicately until the last piece fell.

A tall man sporting a suit coat and tie approached the microphone next. He was clean shaven and meticulously arranged; his hair parted perfectly to the side. His question was brief.

"I have heard you say in the past that property acquisition is the meaning of life and freedom; a right entitled to us in the United States.

"But, you also stated that the government's intent is the control of our property as a pathway to our enslavement. Could you elaborate further on this line of thinking and how it fits in with our ability to maintain this freedom in the United States?"

"Certainly," Lownsbury cast his eyes down in thought before proceeding.

"Let me ask, does anybody here own any personal property?"

Lownsbury vehemently started shaking his head, "People, don't even raise your hands because, no sir you do not," he said pointing to a man down front. "That was a trick question.

"We, as Americans, no longer have a right to own personal property. Property ownership is defined as having absolute control of the property, tangible or intangible, within our personal possession.

"However, that is not our reality. Instead, we pay the government for the ability to *use* property, but we do not fully control it. All we own is speculation or interest in property. An idea so vague that it can be rendered virtually meaningless.

"Consider our largest form of property; Real Estate. Can you decide one day to set fire to your house?"

Lownsbury cast his gaze around before answering his own question, "No, you cannot, because you don't own it; it is not yours to destroy. The order of ownership consists of the government in first place, in perpetuity. As long as they are paid rent in the form of taxes, you can enjoy using and leveraging *their* land, but only to whatever extent they *allow* you.

"We all know the roles of various lending institutions and the order of ownership they posses, but the government will always be in first position. Even if your heirs take on your passing interest, it is the government that needs to be satisfied, and continues to be satisfied for anyone to enjoy the limited use of the property.

"Even your automobiles: You will pay the government when you purchase a car. You may think it belongs to you. Ok, you can think that. In reality your car is merely a hunk of plastic and metal. But, try using that car without continuing to pay the government for the privilege.

"When you later sell that car, you are required to pay the government their cut again. We give the government increasing portions of our property for the privilege to use and leverage the *perception* of property. But, none of our property is ever fully ours.

"Even the smallest bauble that we enjoy," Lownsbury picked up and displayed the push-button bell he had used in his lecture. "The government has its hand in our leverage and use of it. The government controls all aspects of our property. Even our very lives.

"That, ladies and gentlemen, is the definition of slavery, not private property ownership.

"Our government controls our thoughts through propaganda," Lownsbury gestured to the kids outside. "They now have control over our bodies and lives with the takeover of healthcare. And, as the Dregs are perpetuated in another march towards civil war, our souls are now on the line.

"I have said it before, I will say it again," Lownsbury enunciated, "If property ownership is the epitome of freedom and the meaning of life, then slavery is alive and well and most of us are willing participants."

The auditorium fell to a somber silence as the next person approached the microphone.

"Professor Lownsbury," the tall thin man said, as he approached the microphone, "Did I understand you correctly that you said we are all slaves?" His question had a trace of contempt lacing his undertone.

"If you were awake just now, Yes, you certainly heard correctly. However, that is likely not the question you were wanting to ask, so in the interest of time, let me get to the heart of the question you didn't seem to have the wherewithal to ask. You are undoubtedly wondering if I can elaborate on my theories regarding slavery."

The tall man was visibly taken aback, but Lownsbury continued unabated.

"We just had a discussion in which the definition of freedom and the meaning of life is the acquisition of property. And, slavery, therefore, has been defined as the full and total control of someone else's property. Tangible and intangible.

"I think most of us can agree to that definition. If I have control, for example, of this chair, if it is truly my property, that means I can sell it, I can use it, I can give it away, I can destroy it if I wish. I can leverage it, in whatever circumstances can be imagined with that. But, the point is, It is mine to do with as I desire.

"If I look upon another human being as a possession in that manner, It means I have absolute control over his property.

Both tangible and intangible. Absolute control even over his very life.

"Around the world, our governments have positioned themselves in this very same manner. The United States Constitution was written in a way to end this type of control over other people's property; to end slavery. But that concept has always been a pipe dream. So much so, that it was one of the most contentious ideas at the time of its writing. You might as well attempt to end sunshine during daylight hours.

"The dirty secret is there was no real attempt to end it, just a transfer of power from individual citizen owners to the government."

The tall thin man was shaking his head vehemently. "That is not true, Lincoln ended slavery, it was why the Civil War was fought."

Lownsbury looked at him in shock, "You believe the civil war was fought to *end* slavery?"

"Of course. It is common knowledge all of us learned in grade school."

Lownsbury cleared his throat. "You should be more specific. What you should have said is *Government Run Public Schools.* You were obviously not here during this lecture, or had fallen asleep. Otherwise you would understand the importance of that distinction.

"Let's consider this scenario, ladies and gentlemen. During the 1920's, the mobs, especially in Chicago and Las Vegas, were the bane of the government's existence. The government decried the mobs' roles in running numbers, in prostitution and in bootlegging. They placed members of the mob on the number one public enemy's list.

"The populace, in many ways, had differing viewpoints. Al Capone, for example was heralded by many as a hero. He sponsored soup kitchens and put people to work. The populace enjoyed playing the numbers in the hopes of winning big, and some of them even did.

"But, what was the government's real reasons for bringing down the mob? Was it their illegal activities?" Lownsbury shook his head. "Al Capone was brought to prison for income tax evasion. It may have been the only thing they could really pin on him, but it was also telling as to the real motivations of the government.

"The government had no intention of ending the mob, they simply were tired of being cut out of the action that the mob was enjoying. Even today, there are still active gangs with no real reason to stop them. Large mob bosses are still in operation, but instead of a private citizen as the head of the organization, it is now the government. The government's main goal was to seize their *fair share*. To put the United States government as supreme boss over all the other mob bosses.

"It has been proven that the government controls drug trade and allows citizens to play the numbers. We call it lottery now, but the game is still the same." Lownsbury raised his eyebrows, "A game that is miraculously now legal as long as they're in charge.

"The government collects huge taxes on the consumption of alcohol, and *Protection Money* paid by businesses is now euphemistically called their *Fair Share* of tax revenue, but the method of collection has not changed and penalties for not paying are still in place.

"As we can see, the operations are still the same. Many of the activities of the old mob are now considered legal now that the government is in charge. It is only the echelon of control that has changed.

"So, let's put this in context with slavery. It wasn't the institution of slavery the government wanted to end. Slavery is still in existence in greater numbers than it ever was.

"As we have demonstrated with this exercise, it is the absolute power over the citizenry that is the desire. And, the only thing that was brought to an end in 1865 was the private citizen's control of slaves. The private citizen was simply subordinated to the government.

"Consider that I, as the politician in our little demonstration today, have staked claim to all forms of currency among the Producers. And, I can, on a whim, confiscate all that they possess. Their lives. Their property.

"During the 1940's, Franklin Roosevelt outlawed the physical possession of gold, confiscating it from every citizen. The government can confiscate all your belongings, your home, even your children if it so desires. It consistently confiscates your currency for the purpose of giving a portion. A portion they do not skim from the top, mind you, to someone else. Again, for no other reason than political aspirations.

"And, regardless of what they try to convince you of, the government can confiscate your firearms if they so choose. At this point, they do not worry about it much as they know their military can still outgun the populace. That is why their concern is not so much with individuals owning a gun, but making sure that the guns the public do own are not equal to the military's weaponry. It gives the populace a pacifier, allowing them to mistakenly think that portions of those six pages of rules are still in force. But, if they think that the populace may pose a danger to them and their power, they begin to piecemeal the confiscation of those weapons."

Lownsbury offered a quiet laugh.

"My friends, that is the very definition of slavery. We are, all of us, enslaved to our government. It is a form of benign slavery, but slavery nonetheless.

"The south was not so upset over the ending of slavery; slavery was on the verge of ending on its own. They were upset over the government seizing such a huge portion of the southern economy.

"Like healthcare today. It was arguably a large swath of the economy the government seized that upset the apple cart.

"Slavery has always been a part of mankind's nature. There is no end to it. It is the *Slavery Syndrome: Mankind will always allow and nurture the institution of slavery.*

"The history of slavery is as old as man itself. It is such a part of human nature, that people have always been willing participants."

The tall man was shaking his head, "That sounds rather racists. Don't you see how that viewpoint is degrading to African-Americans?"

"Why?" Lownsbury reacted, "I consider your viewpoint nothing more than government sponsored propaganda and that, sir, is degrading to all of us here," he said with a level of vitriol.

"Black Americans do not own the title of slave. Slavery, like slave owners, know no skin color and it does not differentiate between sexes. That is simply political propaganda.

"Neither, are slavery and racism synonymous. They are two distinct terms. We were talking of slavery and its definition. Racism is a divide between two different races of people, often exploited by the politicians for political means and ends. Its definition changing at the whim of the Rule-Makers in efforts to keep division among the populace, and most often used as tools and weapons of misdirection in a person's climb to power. Any time the word, *racism* is bandied, I look at it with a jaundiced eye. The term is far overused, and usually incorrectly for the reasons just stated. In many cases, it cannot be taken seriously."

"But, back in the day, people of the south would refer to black men as inferior. Slavery was held together with racism," the tall man argued.

"Terminology fostered by the politicians," Lownsbury countered. "Terminology that was, and still is, brandished as a political weapon.

"Any time one of these demagogues on television say, *'We must have an open conversation about racism'* I have to laugh," Lownsbury stated. "The setting in which the phrase is used is done so within a situation or a conversation that is already occurring. Therefore, the phrasing is intended to infer that *'Unless you agree with me and my beliefs, the conversation is not occurring or real'*.

Lownsbury paced easily as he continued.

"Many of us in our day to day lives intermingle. We have friends, acquaintances, lovers and spouses of differing races and backgrounds. We listen to the talking heads in the media and in our capital buildings, speaking of this mysterious epidemic of racism, and conclude it must be occurring in towns and neighborhoods other than our own because it just doesn't seem to be manifest. Only those select few of our population that seem to be so hyper-sensitive as to see a boogey man around every corner appear to be affected by this otherwise invisible monster.

"Racism has become a non-sequitur. It has lost most of its relevance. It is now a terminology used to instantly stifle a conversation rather than promote it. Referring to someone as a racist will instantly result in retreat and therefore a minor battle can be claimed.

"Racism is fostered by our leaders. As a populace, we mimic, we parrot, we ape our leaders. And, it is their propaganda that perpetuates racism.

"If you are serious, sir," Lownsbury said, addressing the question asker, "about finding the root cause of racism, you need look no further than our Rule-Makers.

"It is why I personally don't shrink from the word for I do not blindly follow a leader. I will not have the uneducated, mindless drones dictate my personal beliefs or nullify my superb intellect.

"I have given you far more time than you deserve," Lownsbury said to the tall man, dismissing him. "Next question, please."

Another protestor ambled to the microphone. His audacious manner of dress arriving long before his person.

"Yes, Mr. Lownsbury," he drawled with a level of disrespect, "Did I understand you correctly that homosexuals are dregs of society engaged in sin? Many homosexuals I know are business men or members of society just like you."

Lownsbury rubbed his forehead as mild applause of the question dwindled quickly.

"Let me clarify this mystique surrounding the deadly sin of Lust within the Dregs and the meaning and purpose of its advancement, in all its various forms, including homosexuality," Lownsbury began, taking a sip of water from his glass.

"Sex is an overwhelming fact of life among every species of this planet. Procreation is a driving force behind survival of every life form, that has ever lived. But, nature will hold in check the numbers of population of varying species in a variety of ways.

"Many life forms have only a small window of opportunity in which to mate, and because of that, the females of the species must be very selective of the male to ensure healthy offspring."

Lownsbury paused, his stare traveling across the crowd.

"Except for man."

He resumed in his natural cadence, "Some life forms are prolific in their breeding, just as we are, but nature provides sustenance to other animals in the food chain by this proliferation."

Again he expertly paused letting his words penetrate.

"Except with man.

"Nature will instead attempt other methods of population control with mankind from disease, and disasters, to pitting us against each other with war, and genocide," Lownsbury pointed, referencing back to his Bowtie Graphic.

"And, just as nature will assist other species with promulgation by altering their sexual behaviors, so too, it will use our own sexual proclivities for, or against us to manage our own numbers," he paused again, pointing to the garishly dressed man as he let the impact of his implication take hold.

"In other words," Lownsbury said with a long, loud sigh, "The percentage of the population that considers themselves something other than heterosexual is an aberration. With the numbers of Dregs that are stretching their proscribed boundaries, that aberration has become a means by which nature is attempting to control our numbers. A deviation to the natural procreation process has become nature's attempt to bring our population under control.

"Always remember, nature will eventually be victorious. And, whether it is sexual proclivities, or other socialistic anomalies that, as we determined, will eventually lead to genocide, nature will win."

The man squinted his eyes, fuming with obvious hatred.

Lownsbury ignored his scathing stare, continuing, "Let me also add further observation to my theories in relation to this subject."

The man sneered contemptuously in reply.

"Infant mortality used to be one of nature's method of population control," Lownsbury resumed unscathed. "This fact forced the females of our species to be very discriminating in their choice of mate, to ensure the best chance for survival of their offspring. But, as time went on, mankind successfully counteracted this natural balance.

"We commonly believe that we live longer today than what we used to. That our life expectancy is growing as our technology progresses. We believe this because that is what we are told. And, to some degree, modern medicine has indeed lengthened our lifespan.

"But, what has changed more than anything to give us our increasing life expectancy averages is infant mortality numbers. The infant mortality numbers has declined through the years, and along with it, women's discrimination with mate choices.

"The decline of discretion by the women in this manner, forced mankind's creation of societal *mores* to provide natural population control. This included traditions surrounding procreation and family, marriage, societal castigation for poor decisions and indiscretions and the inclusion of Lust as part of the seven deadly sins. Mankind has always instinctually, albeit reluctantly, understood the need to check themselves, and this came to embody the instruction of etiquette to young ladies.

"In other words, there were reasons behind teaching women to act like ladies and men to act like gentlemen that went beyond simple decorum. It was viewed as a means to survival.

"As time progressed further and the infant mortality rate went into the single digits, the decline of moral values within our society directly mirrored these advancements.

"The invention of the birth control pill finally gave license to women to throw away the constraints of traditional dictates and etiquette as nearly every child born in the modern day achieves adulthood.

"Much to the delight of men, morality and decorum have fallen to the wayside as the virtues of women have all but been forgotten. This has caused a tremendous spike in population, especially among the Dregs, and an ongoing protraction of the seven deadly sins.

"Instinctually, we enjoy being unconstrained by morality. We enjoy the freedoms of abandon without consequence. But, intellectually, the wisest among us know there can be no such thing. Eventually, nature will check us.

"We learn that nature is all around us. And, even as we attempt to fight against it, and even come to believe we are winning, we find that the fight is still a natural occurrence with an inevitable outcome.

"Man will always sow the seeds of his own destruction, even as he reaps the harvest of his own success.

"Our ancestors understood this concept, but collective amnesia is a powerful aphrodisiac and it becomes a lesson that needs to be relearned from time to time.

"Unfortunately, it is often a harsh lesson."

As Lownsbury retrieved his water glass again, he made a dismissive gesture with his hand, ending the discussion.

The look of vitriol on the ostentatious man's face lingered long after he stormed from the hall, and I couldn't help but laugh.

A young man with glasses, also a protestor, approached the microphone. "Thank you, Doctor Lownsbury. It is a consensus among the scientific community that Global Climate change is occurring and that man is the leading cause of the damage. With the advocacy of your *Rainmaker Syndrome*, does that mean you do not believe in global climate change?"

Lownsbury leaped right into his answer, " Your preamble did you quite the disservice. You cleverly start with a premise. A mistaken one, mind you. Then, proceed with a question that is based on that erroneous belief. It would do you well, young man, to discover your facts before trying your hand at debating a subject of which you obviously know very little."

"I don't understand..." the question asker began.

"I know," Lownsbury quickly answered.

"It is widely believed among the populace that a general consensus exists among the scientists that global climate change is occurring. For as much as you can believe there to be consensus in actual scientific theory," Lownsbury continued, "The phrasing is nonetheless misleading to the populace at large."

He explained, "Many scientists will agree that the climate has been changing since the earth first formed. Ice ages encroaching and retreating in cyclical patterns. Sunspots randomly affecting atmospheric changes throughout our eco system, volcanoes opening holes in the ozone, etcetera.

"This is most likely the general consensus that is referred to, and the terminology of which that is used in a misleading fashion.

"Where the divergence of so-called consensus occurs is to the degree of which man is having an effect to that ongoing climate change." Lownsbury shrugged, "Perhaps, we are. I really wouldn't doubt it. But, it is a much further leap of illogic to believe that man has any ability to affect the issue in a different manner. Especially without a drastic population reduction.

"This is the concept I refer to as the *Rainmaker Syndrome*.

"Since man first planted a seed in the earth and willed it grow, he has had a desire to affect nature to his own benefit.

"It is the unscrupulous Rule-Makers, as we have learned, that capitalize on that mistaken belief. They preach that man can indeed cause the sky to rain and the sun to shine at that perfect temperature anywhere they want around the globe. And, falsely promise this ability in an effort to possess ever increasing power over the populace. To enslave all of us ever further by using the token Philosophers, such as Phil the Scientist and Phil the Teacher, as pawns to promulgate myths for the purpose of perpetuating the Rule-Maker's power.

"The promise of perfect climate control is nonsensical and it is at that very heart that our scientists disagree. You will find that, more often than not, it is the scientists that possess grants from the Rule-Makers that insist we can perform a rain dance to achieve climate perfection.

"Those scientist's that do not receive money from the Rule-Makers are typically the ones that dissent as to the opinions of their so-called contemporaries. It is all part and parcel of my *Scientific Syndrome*."

The young man was stubborn, "So, do you think we should continue to pollute the planet? Shouldn't the government mandate pollution controls to at least attempt to prevent global climate change?"

Lownsbury shook his head, "Your ignorance runs deep. You again offer two false premises blended into one. No one is advocating for polluting this planet. There may be a handful of people that are indifferent, but pollution and climate change are two separate issues. The argument emerges as to how much control over your life the government has. Submit all you want, sir, but how dare you force the rest of us to submit to having our freedoms stripped from us. I will not willingly offer up myself for enslavement because of *your* ignorant, misguided beliefs. I have already stated my contempt at that idea.

"You are dismissed."

A heavy set man breathed harshly into the microphone, "Professor, You said that cops and criminals are two sides of the same coin. That they have similar mentalities and viewpoints; that it is only a matter of circumstance that differentiates them. So, am I to understand that you believe cops and soldiers to be in the same category as thieves and law breakers?"

Lownsbury smiled, "My theories surrounding Tom the Thief always generates incredulity and misunderstanding."

Rubbing his chin in thought, Lownsbury began his casual pacing, "I agree that it can be a hard concept to follow, so let me try to clarify.

"The actual rule surrounding our player, Tom, is this. If Tom is sanctioned by our Producers and more importantly, the Rule-Maker, then Tom is a hero.

"If Tom works alone, to his own benefit or to a private individual or even as a hero on an opposing tribe, Tom is considered a villain.

"Both sides of Tom's token have the same job description, and that is to steal, or take away the property of Producers. Remember, this includes a person's life, their time, or their possessions. Be they on opposing tribes, or within their own tribe. Thus, I have given this double-sided token the title of thief.

"For example, let's look at the highest ranking thief among our hero side of the token; a soldier. Many times, a soldier will be set on a course to invade or defend against an opposing tribe. An honorable endeavor, to be sure.

"Sometimes though, he is even tasked to attack his own tribe," Lownsbury offered a perfectly timed pause letting this idea settle.

"Our soldier will often fight against the equally ranked, opposing villain. But, if the goal of the battle is victory, they often times will have to take the lives or possessions of a large number of the other tribe's Producer's."

The large question asker interrupted with a heavy breath, "Are you saying it should be army practice to kill innocent civilians?" his tone was incredulous.

Lownsbury tilted his head, "If the goal is victory then, yes. It has always been known that the best way to defeat an enemy is to break their supply chain. That supply chain stems from one main source: the Producers. Wipe them from the picture, or even just demoralize them, and you can often force a surrender.

"Otherwise, you are engaged in a war without end. A war devised with another goal entirely than that of victory. A goal typically designed for the benefit of the Rule-Maker.

"That goal can be wealth production, such as through some form of charity scam; Military practice; or a show of force to others. Whatever the ultimate goal is, it is usually something other than victory.

"Our present enemies understand this. It is why they train to kill civilians. Many times more so than training to fight on the battlefield.

"Unfortunately, for us, this is a strategy that could bring about their success.

"Surgical strikes on our part may work to a point, but until you start wiping out the other side's production population, it's very possible you will not be fully successful. This is an unfortunate reality that all soldiers throughout history have understood.

"Let's bring that line of thought down to our cities. We have a small number of ranking police officers that are chosen to confront an equally ranking villain in an effort to control chaos.

"Revenue is collected at ever increasing rates from the producers for this endeavor; the supply chain. But, the problem remains unsolved and, as dictated with the Charity Scam Syndrome, remains a problem that the Rule-Makers have no desire to solve.

"However, there is not as much money to be made in confronting those villains in comparison to taking the Producer's money directly for minor infractions. So, the lowest ranking police officers have become designated revenue collectors for the Rule-Makers.

"Rule-Makers will make enough laws so that every citizen becomes a criminal, and the property of the Producers can be confiscated for any infraction the officers manage to witness."

"I take great exception to that," the large man breathed into the microphone, shaking his head, his voice nearly cracking with emotion, "My son is a cop and I appreciate the police and what they have to deal with. They have a difficult and necessary job in protecting and serving."

"I agree," Lownsbury responded, his eyebrows raising. "I do not believe I said anything to the contrary. The police have tremendous obstacles to deal with. But, unfortunately, these obstacles are, in large part, put in place by their benefactors; the Rule-Makers.

"But, let's look at what you just said about an officer's duty to Protect and Serve.

"The only way the police can protect the public is by removing from the population, the villains that intend public harm. But, it is up to the Rule-Makers to keep the villains in jail or otherwise remove them from society, and that costs money. Money that many villains do not have."

Lownsbury paused and drifted his gaze, "But, the Producer's do.

"Unfortunately, the Producers are not inclined to be an unending supply of money for harmless people caught up in the system, or violent villains that will never be able to join the population and are instead destined to live out their lives without want and on the Producer's dime.

"But, keeping these perpetually violent criminals alive is paramount to a Rule-Maker receiving a never ending supply of money from the Producers. A classic and transparent dilemma.

"On the other hand, there is literally no way that the police can protect the rest of the public at large if these dangerous villains are not removed from the picture. It is not possible. An officer would have to be at the right place, at the right time, always. Protection of the individual has to be done individually. And, with the use of deadly force if necessary."

"The big man nodded his head in understanding, "I completely understand that the use of deadly force in the protection of oneself has been made criminal, and that it is a problem fostered by our Rule-Makers. Most cops agree with our Constitution."

"Absolutely right," Lownsbury continued, "It is why, in my mind, our Rule-Makers refer to our justice system as *Criminal Justice*, rather than *Victim Justice.*"

Lownsbury resumed, "The issue of the police *Serving* the public has been also been rendered obsolete.

"It used to be that a mild infraction would lead to an officer admonishing rather than punishing. Helping the public is usually an officer's true desire, but again, the Rule-Makers have taken that freedom of serving the public away from the officer.

"By dictating mandatory sentencing and punishment, the Rule-Makers have effectively removed any discretion from the officers and judges. By imposing penalties and confiscation of the producer's property for the mildest of infractions increases revenue and power to the Rule-Makers.

"Unfortunately, this policy also creates discord among the populace against the *bearer of bad news*: the police. This is why we have seen the ire of the public turn negative to the police as of late. It is the Rule-Makers mindless short-sightedness when they create endless rules and regulation that they will never relinquish. The Rule-Maker's egos will never allow them to see the errors of their ways while their wallets continue to expand.

"Most police officers are heroes because they want to help people, but they come to understand quickly that their benefactor's are not so inclined. The ***Benefactor Syndrome*** allows them little say in the matter.

"As the ire of the public increases in tandem with the ongoing authoritarian rules, they will come to see the police as enemies. Naturally, the police will reciprocate with justification in each officer's mind for criminalizing the public.

"It is a vicious cycle that will generally see a violent end when the Rule-Makers are finally forced from power, and put back into their constitutional constraints."

Lownsbury brought his discussion to a quick end, "I hope I was clear in my explanation, and I want to stress this is not an indictment of our heroes; this is indictment of our Rule-Makers, pulled from the dregs. Rule-Makers that create losing situations among all of the Producers and Tokens for their own selfish pursuits."

The large man nodded his head and breathed a heavy sigh, "Yes, you have professor. Thank you."

I had the impression that the question asker now approaching the microphone, would offer a smarmy diatribe before eventually fielding a typically inane question. The purposeful stride to the microphone seemed to enunciate an underlying contemptuous conceit. A narcissistic aura that radiated from his every pore. But I was pleasantly surprised that his question was a simple request for clarification. Clarification of an item I had hoped for as well.

"Thank you professor. I have been leafing through your ***Syndromes of Civilization*** page, and I see this one labeled here as the **Egg Syndrome**, Could you offer some insight as to what that syndrome is and what it means to you?"

Lownsbury scratched his eyebrow before furrowing it in thought.

"The *Egg Syndrome* reads as this: *Every scientist's findings should be viewed with a jaundiced eye, especially if the scientist is financed by government. For those findings will change tomorrow and the next.*

"There are a plethora of examples throughout our history cataloging the untrustworthiness of scientific findings. Especially those spawned by research conducted through government sponsorship. No finer example of this phenomena can be found than in the research that has been conducted surrounding the simple chicken egg.

"It was revealed through much pomp and circumstance, a number of years ago, that the egg was considered the most harmful food that a person could eat. Brimming with deadly cholesterol, it promised to stop a beating heart within seconds of its ingestion.

"An unsettling judgment of the time that only seemed to be rivaled by another scientific certainty that we were all doomed to freeze to death due to global cooling and the encroachment of a fast moving ice age." Lownsbury laughed, "Man caused, of course.

"These revered findings surrounding the egg came as a surprise to many of our elderly grandparents who had eaten eggs every day of their lives. But, the naive, younger generations believed these so-called scientific conclusions just as surely as they did the impending arrival of the next glacial epoch.

"On the heels of this unsettling discovery concerning everyone's favorite breakfast food, came the news that it wasn't the entire egg that was harmful, it was only the egg yolks that were to be blamed for their poisonous qualities. Egg white omelets were suddenly all the rage.

"Back and forth this see-saw of scientific certainty would oscillate. Decrying and then redeeming every step of the egg's delivery and cooking process to an otherwise uninformed public. Revealing the bleak reality of the next coming plague residing within each white, thin shelled ovum.

"Then, recently, as if by magic, a wonderful secret was discovered that our grandparents seemed to have been wise to all along. And, now we can all rest easy, ladies and gentlemen. As of today, our wonderful egg is regarded as the world's perfect food."

A quick bout of laughter came and went and the professor continued, "The scenario I have described surrounding the history of egg research is only a small example of the cycle of castigation and redemption in all forms of government sponsored research programs proselytized to the public on a daily basis."

Lownsbury tilted his head with a look of thoughtfulness, "But, what is the reasoning behind this cycle surrounding the egg? Why and how can a simple food, such as the egg, be the subject of such unmitigated scrutiny? Castigated and redeemed time and again to an ignorant public that accept blindly the next ramblings of the government sponsored scientific community?"

Lownsbury touched a finger to his lips as he maneuvered lightly on his feet.

"A number of possible reasons have been suggested. For instance, Lobby money competing for room in our Rule-Maker's pockets from the grain farmers and then conversely the poultry farmers, have been offered as an explanation. And, as we have demonstrated here today, that line of thought can be considered a reasonable premise.

"As we know, any business that offers the Rule-Maker the most money will receive favorable treatment from the government sponsored scientist. It is a known fact.

"But, one other thing is also certain: The scientists that have been studying all of the various research projects, like the egg, have been paid billions of dollars through the years and given a never ending job to conduct this research. Meanwhile, the Rule-Maker will happily continue to put the line item of egg research on the government's balance sheet and collect that dollar from every producer for the revelation of the next discovery du jour."

"Are you saying that no government research should be considered reliable?" The question asker tilted his head, "That seems outlandish and naive as well."

"What I am saying, Lownsbury said softly, "Is that the findings of any scientist, especially those paid by the government, should be taken with grain of salt. I would much more be inclined to believe a privately funded scientific community than anyone that is beholden to a Rule-Maker."

"Yes professor, I was wondering if you would delve into the history of the United States and how your demonstration today relates?" The older, portly lady, very well dressed asked quietly. Her voice radiated a sweetness that was undoubtedly a representation of her entire persona.

Lownsbury smiled, we all did.

"The history of the World, in many ways is a mirror image of the history of the United States. We will typically study all the important figures and dates as part of our education in history. But, the main history of the United States can summarily be divided into four parts. These include:"

Lownsbury counted them off using his fingers, "The events leading up to the Revolutionary War.

"The after effects of revolution, and the subsequent events that led up to the Civil War.

"The after effects of Civil War and the subsequent events leading up to World War Two.

"The effects of that war and our current period leading us to our second Civil War.

"Each one of these steps are very similar in cause, effect, and outcome. Only individual occurrences and anecdotes differentiate them, but they are all so similar as to be able to predict outcomes of the future."

Lownsbury was talking to the audience at large, "Each one of these steps proceed and proceeded in this fashion:

"The ruling government amasses increasing power. By definition, the more power the government has, the less power the people have over their own lives. Eventually, the people's desire for individual freedom peaks until armed conflict results. The armed conflict produces a perceived victor, and in all these cases, as with every case throughout history, the victor is, or becomes a governing force. That government once again starts the march towards removing freedoms from the people. Increasing its power until, once again, the people reach a breaking point and attempt to take out their leaders, and in many cases, violently so."

Lownsbury took a sip of water and set his glass on the table next to the receptionist bell.

"The founding fathers perceived this pattern. A pattern not exclusive to the United States, rather one prevalent in all of World History. They wrote the Constitution in an attempt to prevent this ongoing occurrence. An attempt to guarantee the American people power over their government.

"But, government and politicians are never resigned to live within their confinements. They must grow. Nature dictates their growth and their march towards a genocidal outcome. You can have a hundred Constitutions limiting their power in all manners and Rule-Makers will find a way to circumvent them. It is inevitable.

"So how does that equate with the war on terrorism?" the sweet, old lady asked.

"The chain of events I have just described is an aside from the fact that civilizations throughout the history of the world have always had to deal with barbarians at the gate. Barbarians are an annoyance that will sometimes even conquer an individual civilization from time to time. But, when the overall populations of the world have had enough, they typically will beat them back.

"Unfortunately, it is not a pleasant task because in order to accomplish that, civilized people have to steel themselves for the task of utter annihilation of the offenders. Not an easy concept to accept, much less employ.

"But, as my *Barbarian Syndrome* details, there will always be barbarians that the civilized world has to deal with in tandem with their own repeating pathways of self-inflicted wounds that I refer to as the *Suicide Syndrome.*"

Five

Epiphany

The question and answer session continued for several more minutes, but my mind was drifting inward by now.

The elusive epiphany that had plagued me during the Professor's lecture was beginning to become clear. I could see how Lownsbury's theories and philosophies could be viewed as incendiary by some. Especially to those who would choose subservience to their emotions and close their minds to compelling avenues of thought.

Yet, I could not deny the truth in many of the assertions the professor had made. I began to realize that to deny the truth and to hide in the darkness of politically correct euphemisms, led one into the acceptance of malevolent propaganda. It was tantamount to snapping closed the chains of bondage on oneself as surely as if another who held dominion over you was to do.

But, to place yourself in that kind of bondage was a sin even more hideous than that of a slaver. To enslave oneself in the mask of desirable dialogue; to remove yourself from thoughtfulness and plain speak was a far greater sin; an unforgiveable travesty to oneself.

Yet, I could see that to some, this was an easier road than pulling back the veil of truth.

I could understand the vitriolic apathy of so many people when confronted with these types of viewpoints. I now understood why so many historical figures, who had also preached these timeless concepts, had been vilified.

To cast off political dogma and embrace, or at least entertain, viewpoints such as Doctor Lownsbury's and his *Syndromes of Civilization*, also dictated a need for deep introspection of oneself. A difficult, if not impossible undertaking for the great unwashed.

I had come to realize that self-enslavement to the Rule-Maker's propaganda was, to so many, the path of least resistance. A pathway of ignorant desirability, and therefore one so often travelled.

Perhaps this was the epiphany I was meant to see.

Six

Epilogue

I was unable to talk to the professor after the lecture. The throng milling about him was intense. He was virtually drowning in a sea of people.

I saw the usher expertly dividing the hand-grabbers from the riff-raff as people swarmed through and from the auditorium.

I handed the usher my card with a brief description hastily scribbled on the back; an offer to write a fair expose on Lownsbury and his philosophies. If the professor would grant an audience to discuss this possibility, I would be grateful.

The usher deposited the card, mindlessly, in the pocket of his vest with a promise to deliver the message. His attention immediately became hostage elsewhere and I left the auditorium hopeful, yet discontent.

Months went by and my discontentment turned to disappointment when I had yet to receive any word from Professor Lownsbury.

I was becoming increasingly disenchanted with the news agency of which I was associated. Virtually overnight they had degraded into a tabloid paper mill, taking positions in line with the archetypical propaganda spewed by growing masses across the land.

I also became unable to tolerate the ostracization from my co-workers for daring to take to heart some of the theories I had learned that evening listening to Doctor Lownsbury. His lecture concerning the *Syndromes of Civilization* had resonated with me, and I was becoming increasingly adept at recognizing the true ignorance of those I encountered in my day to day life.

It was some months later when I was awakened from a deep sleep. The alarm clock indicated that it was one o'clock in the morning.

I instantly recognized the voice on the other end of the line. The soft, South African English was silky smooth. My heart skipped a measure and I instantly snapped awake as my hopes rose to an unprecedented level.

I barely heard the question I had been waiting for all these many months. I had to ask him to repeat himself just to be sure I understood correctly, and I found myself agreeing to a meeting with him to begin work on a writing assignment.

I was excited. I already had most of the outline for the work you have just read. I merely needed his editing ideas and final approval, and I could have a published work inside of a month. I was certain I was on the verge of an exclusive.

I immediately quit my job with the paper for I had no desire to share my work with such a mindless group of backwards thinking people. I only had to tolerate one last smirk of contempt from them that next morning. None of us shed a tear over my parting.

I flew to London that same morning, teetering on the edge of nirvana. I had played scenarios through my head during the entire flight, as I stared absently at the ocean far below, envisioning Doctor Lownsbury reading my manuscript. His own excitement mounting at having his lecture published for the first time. I truly thought I was riding the crest of a building wave that would shake the foundations of every establishment when it came ashore.

The British library was as a tomb when I finally arrived. There was absolutely no one around. The door had opened easily enough, but it clicked shut behind me with an ominous tone. I tested the handle and found the lock had mysteriously engaged.

It was the eeriest of feelings walking easily through the wide open hallways. The massive architecture was intimidating; the grand rotunda and its massive colonnades. Having such a beautiful and infamous building to oneself sent waves of vertigo washing through me. I was growing increasingly certain that I was not supposed to be there. That I had fallen for some elaborate hoax.

I had no idea what I was looking for. I had not been instructed any further than to make it to, and inside the library. I was thinking perhaps of finding a hotel, if I could find a way out, and returning during a timeframe where staff would be available to offer me guidance.

When I came across a door.

The sign above it indicated it was the entrance to the stairwell, but a sticky note posted in the middle of the door had my name on it.

Pushing through the door I could see a staircase to my left and an elevator door to my right. Another door stood directly opposite and appeared to open into another section of the library.

With no other direction, I made for the opposite door. As I passed by the elevator, the compartment door suddenly slid open. There were no passengers inside the compartment, and that familiar feeling of vertigo played through me once again.

I realized that I was being watched and directed through a great deal of subterfuge.

I stepped into the elevator car, and the doors closed behind me. The elevator immediately began to ascend on its own and my feeling of vertigo turned to one of claustrophobia. I was overtaken with panic, and began stabbing randomly, and in vain, at the elevator car buttons. It seemed like an eternity passed before the car came to a gentle stop.

Behind me the doors opened into splendor.

The room that greeted me was well beyond what a library should be.

This... this was something different.

Masterpieces from ages long past adorned the walls. Paintings and sculptures from the masters reached into every corner. Their magnificence dictating them to be originals.

I was awe struck as I stared around the room. Piece after piece stabbed my eyes with their brilliance. Bookshelves swelled with titles and bindings that would undoubtedly wed perfectly with the other masterpieces that filled the room.

Lownsbury appeared, as if by magic among the treasure. He crossed easily across a small foyer to greet me, and offered me a cup of tea.

I graciously accepted, still stricken at the enormity of what I was witness to. Although, the room had a grandeur that would be difficult to equal. Lownsbury's own presence seemed to fit in neatly with the majesty of the museum quality gala.

I became even more overwhelmed, if it was possible, for I could not get over the depth of the professor's eyes. It was like looking into a well of timelessness.

Of wisdom.

I shook my head to remove my obvious bleariness caused by the jet lag. I had been witness to a massive amount of sensory input, and was still trying to deal with everything that had transpired since my one am wake up call.

Lownsbury allowed me a moment for composure, and then offered to give me a tour around the large room.

He gave me brief instruction about the artwork. How his collection held all original's. Masterpieces from Monet, Rembrandt, Michelangelo - pieces that I never knew existed. Created by the masters themselves, but never placed on public display.

Lownsbury eventually steered us to a small sitting area with a low table. Taking our seats, we began to talk.

My excitement was omnipresent as I showed him a transcript of his lecture. Written with as much detail and flair as I could manage, without sounding too overdone. Much of it admittedly from memory.

We sat in silence as he read, flipping through the pages casually.

I was hopeful as I awaited his response, but that hopefulness began to dwindle as the speed of which he turned through the pages increased.

I was re-running through my scenarios of his response. Hoping with every fiber for his acceptance and blessing of what he read. Trying to steer him with my mental power alone for his praise.

But, what he said next was a cold slap in my face.

The last few pages of the manuscript remained unread. He had barely skimmed the last section. There was no way he had been able to read it in its entirety and he seemed to have actually become bored with it.

"I do not necessarily need you to write about my philosophies," he said dismissively, throwing the manuscript onto the low coffee table. "These concepts and philosophies are no different as to many of those that came before me. They are not new ideas. They are becoming tiring tripe."

"But, America..." I began to whine.

Lownsbury held up his hand, ending my tirade before it began.

"The American civilization will follow its own course. Just as history has dictated with other civilizations, regardless of what I have to say about it," he shook his head. "I have something else in mind entirely."

I was deflated. Jet lag seemed to make it worse. I ran my hand through my hair, thinking I might just explode with emotion.

"I just needed to meet with you in person and affirm that your writing style comports well with my own, so as to detail a version of events for your transcription." he said with a condescending smile.

"I have known of you for a long time," Lownsbury said mysteriously, smiling at my obvious exasperation. "You can publish this work with my blessing," he said with a level of detachment, waving his hand at the manuscript that now lay rather unceremoniously upon the coffee table.

"If you don't want me to write about your lectures, what do you want," I nearly cried. I had been through a roller coaster of emotion, and I was suddenly exhausted.

Lownsbury's eyes narrowed, as he slid forward in his seat. He settled his teacup on the table.

"Have you ever wondered about the true origin of man?" he said breathlessly. His voice dropping to a whisper. "Where we all came from, originally?" his fingers touched in that form of emphasis I had come to know so well sitting through his lecture.

"Have you ever wanted to know the deepest mysteries of the universe and be able to see through the eyes of the most intense and impactful historical figures to have walked this planet? To have the answers to some of history's most intriguing questions?"

I was initially confused by his questioning. But, his words were spoken with such unbridled intensity, I could not help but find a new level of intrigue as the seconds unfolded.

Lownsbury's eyes flashed and I could see an even further deepening into the vastness of this man's intellect. An unfathomable timelessness and wisdom that radiated from his stare. He seemed to shimmer in the fading sunlight, the rays of which glinted upon some of mankind's most guarded treasures in that regal library.

I cast my gaze through the artifacts of centuries gone by. An unprecedented testament to civilizations and people that had come and gone. A legacy of time and history.

Serendipitous.

He gave the smallest of smiles as I contemplated my answer.

There was only one response I could even think to make.

"Tell me..."

Chapter Excerpt From

The Machine; First Strike

On The Road To Monument, Present Day

"Déjà vu, man."

Captain Jack Sterling saw the cow just as Will Masters uttered the words.

"Déjà vu, man."

A tingle of anxiety coursed through him like an electric shock. Sterling's vision swam amidst a tide of vertigo. He, too was having a serious feeling of reliving this moment. An aching desire to direct his two men to do something different was pulling at him, almost as if nature wanted…

No!

Needed, them to be on a different path.

Sterling twisted in his seat and peered out the back window.

A police cruiser had just turned out onto the county road behind them.

Although the officer had not activated his flashers, it was evident that he intended to give pursuit.

Turning back around, Sterling caught sight of another cruiser making haste towards their position from the west.

He thought it rather curious at how rapidly they had mobilized, but the thought evaporated as quickly as it had formed.

Jack Sterling decided a new course of action.

"Don't turn into the parking lot," he commanded, "We got cops on our tail."

Masters looked into his rearview mirror, a wave of panic was visibly washing over him at the sight of the police cruisers.

"Take the highway," Sterling instructed, "Do it quickly."

Masters kept the car pointed straight, blazing through the yellow light and onto the entrance ramp of I-25 heading south to Colorado Springs.

"Don't you think we should pull to the side?" Lownsbury cautioned. "I mean they haven't even put their lights on yet, they may not even be after us."

"They will be," Sterling said confidently, examining his time phone. He ran his fingers across the keypad, attempting to recall Masters' instructions for setting the coordinates.

No sooner had the words, *"They will be,"* escaped Sterling's lips, than the emergency beacons on the two pursuing patrol cars came to life.

"You better hit the gas, Cowboy," Sterling said with a measured level of calm.

Masters' reaction was instant. Mashing the accelerator to the floor, the car exploded onto the highway. From the front passenger seat, Lownsbury started making mewling noises as their car rocketed down the highway.

As if from nowhere, the afternoon suddenly erupted with police and sheriffs' vehicles giving chase.

"I don't believe this is a proper course of action," Lownsbury complained, clinging desperately to the handle above his door.

A large helicopter could suddenly be heard thundering overhead, flying very low.

Sterling was suddenly very concerned; In all of his military experience, he had never witnessed a pursuit transpire so quickly, or aggressively.

"They don't call out helicopters like this for typical pursuit, at least not immediately and definitely not army choppers," Sterling said calmly, again wondering at the reaction time of law enforcement and now a military response. Schulte would have had to have made that call hours ago, he considered. But, how was that possible?

"The senator must be behind this," Sterling said aloud. "If we pull over now, they will likely have to pipe daylight to us. Calm down, Doc and adjust yours and Cowboy's phone for September 21st, 1940."

Lownsbury seemed to regain a level of his composure and managed to start making the entry into one of the phones. He was obviously nervous and his hands shook as he attempted to press the proper buttons. His body was swaying back and forth with the movements of the car and he was having a hard time focusing on the task.

Lownsbury's calm was short lived, however as the car swerved violently onto the shoulder of the highway, narrowly missing a semi tractor trailer. The driver blasted the truck's massive air horn as the Taurus sped by.

"Oh, sweet Jesus!" Lownsbury cried.

"Doc!" Sterling suddenly shouted.

Scooting forward to put himself closer to the middle of the front seat, Sterling grabbed Lownsbury's collar.

"Focus here, Doc. Masters' job is to drive the car. Your job is to get those goddamn numbers into the phones. Stop whining, and get it done. *Now!"*

Lownsbury nervously nodded his assent and once again focused his concentration on the phones.

A loudspeaker suddenly opened up, and they could hear the pilot of the chopper calling to them. His words were muffled and indistinct, but the meaning was clear.

Pull your vehicle over.

"Oh, my God!" Lownsbury moaned, stealing a glance at the speedometer.

The needle was floating well past the one hundred mark.

"We are going to have to get off the highway in order to do this," Sterling observed, "We don't want the car careening down the highway unmanned."

Lownsbury suddenly shouted, his eyes betraying the terror he was undoubtedly feeling.

"These phones are untested! What if they don't work?"

Sterling realized that Lownsbury had never been in this type of situation before, but he needed to get Doc under control.

He brought his nose close to Lownsbury's ear. His whisper harsh and vicious.

"Put in the goddamn numbers!"

"Uh, Cap?" Masters said, gesturing down the highway.

The highway had cleared behind them as cars had pulled to the side of the road, allowing a full formation of police vehicles to spread across the highway.

Ahead of them, the army chopper had sunk low to the highway, causing traffic to come to a standstill. Brake lights were popping on fast and bright.

"Take the exit!" Sterling pointed, but Masters was already jerking the wheel hard to the right.

Swerving at the last minute and cutting across part of the unpaved triangle of the exit ramp, the car bounced heavily across the grassy divider and back onto the pavement. Masters again mashed the pedal to the floor and the engine screamed against the strain.

Sterling could see two police officers huddling behind their cruisers at the top of the exit ramp. Their weapons trained decisively at the rapidly approaching car.

Swerving evasively, Masters instinctively took aim at the narrow gap that separated the two cruisers. Small puffs of spent gunpowder could be seen billowing in front of the two police officer's weapons. But, the imagery remained elusive until the windshield splintered and tiny projectiles of glass showered the interior of the cabin.

Hitting the island hard, Masters expertly swerved the car around and behind one of the cruisers, causing the officer to dive for cover.

As they rocketed across the overpass, Sterling saw the army chopper was back to giving chase. Again, he tried to process the speed at which the pursuit had manifested, but it was hard to comprehend how Schulte, even as a powerful senator, could have managed such a feat.

"We need those phones, Doc!" Sterling impressed, as he tried to bring his attention back to inputting the coordinates into his own phone.

"The car's been hit, Cap!"

Steam was billowing from the front of the car and a quick look at the temperature gauge told Sterling that the radiator had been compromised.

They were down to seconds.

The car shot down a narrow winding road, past an old mining museum and out into the open country side that was rapidly becoming developed.

Sterling could hear the chopper approaching fast and low, settling into a hover about a quarter mile ahead. But, he was having a hard time believing what he was seeing. The chopper's large, fifty caliber guns were bearing down on their position.

They were clearly preparing to open fire!

This had to be a dream. Sterling still could not fathom how fast the whole pursuit had commenced and how aggressive the response was becoming. Schulte had to have some serious connections to allow for this type of hostility. Something about this just didn't make any sense.

The sheriff and police cruisers were quickly dropping back to make sure they would not be in the line of fire from the large caliber weapon.

Sterling began to sweat.

"Doc!"

Lownsbury quickly and quietly handed Masters his phone.

"Do it now!"

The car was still doing well over ninety when Masters suddenly disappeared amidst a deafening roar.

Sterling could see large eruptions of dirt from the road in front of them, spitting high into the air by the heavy weapons fire as the car sped towards the hovering chopper.

Lownsbury looked into the backseat at Sterling and the two men's eyes locked momentarily.

With a blast of air smashing through the interior of the car, Lownsbury vanished.

The beastly rounds from the heavy fifty caliber machine gun began ripping into the body of the car, progressing up the hood as the car sped on.

Sterling saw the windshield explode and the front seats began to disintegrate into puffs of padding and filler.

Sterling pressed the button.

All available oxygen seemed to leave the car at once, and silence engulfed him.

Bits of floating debris became suspended in mid-air. Sterling saw openings forming in the roof of the car as the high caliber rounds continued to rip into, and through the out of control vehicle.

He watched in fascination as a hole slowly formed at an angle in front of him.

A slightly flattened projectile emerged, spinning through the opening it was making. The sheet metal split against the strain, the delicate ceiling fabric tearing as the large round continued lazily spinning towards him.

Sterling watched the round slow, finally coming to a stop.

Hanging still and silent for just a moment.

Frozen in time.

Slowly, it began to reverse direction.

The laws of physics, a mere suggestion as the round began to spin in the opposite direction, floating slowly back to the hole it had originated from.

Amazed, Sterling watched every round which had penetrated the car perform this same miracle. Each projectile, leaping into midair and magically spinning back through the holes they had originally made.

Faster and faster.

Round after round sprung from the floor boards and the upholstery, sealing up the holes as they left the vehicle.

Fabric and stuffing that had been flying around the interior of the car drifted back to the holes in which it had originated.

Faster and faster.

The projectiles soundlessly left the car, the windshield miraculously healing in their wake.

Sterling felt a wave of panic when Masters and Lownsbury suddenly appeared and the whole car was propelled backwards through his body.

Sterling was left hovering slightly above the ground in a sitting position, slowly moving forward. He watched in amazement as bullets that had struck the ground, leaped out of the earth in flight towards the chopper hanging above him.

Faster and faster.

Silently, the chopper flew backwards out of sight.

Sterling noticed, with some alarm, that he could not turn his head to watch its departure. In fact he couldn't move or even breathe.

He struggled to remain calm as time flew by at an ever-increasing speed.

The sun lit up the scenery like a strobe light in a dance hall. Flashing at dizzying speed.

Trees stood up from nowhere and began to shrink.

Winter snow came and went.

Faster and faster.

Summer leaves leapt from the ground and found their way back to their limbs, only to wither to buds.

Over and over again, the seasons changed at blinding speed in front of Sterling's eyes.

Animals blurred by at an alarming pace and sometimes the hazy figure of a human or two emerged.

It became evident he was in the middle of a farmer's field. The paved road that they had been on was now a service road that cut down the middle of this field.

Sterling could not get a fix on the weather as it was constantly changing. No sooner had it started to rain, then it cleared up and, just as quickly, began snowing from the ground up.

Faster.

Sterling was starting to feel the pain in his chest and sides as his brain began to crave oxygen. He could not get his lungs to work and the rest of his body was just as immobilized.

Time was speeding by all around him at an alarming rate with no signs of slowing and he began to wonder if the trip would ever end.

Panic was on the verge of setting in. His lungs were screaming for air and he could do nothing about it.

He noticed he was still holding the time phone in his left hand and it was blinking madly.

The blinking light on the phone only seemed to intensify the panic he was feeling and he did his best to ignore it.

Faster.

The stroboscopic effect, caused by the sun flashing by at high speed became unbearable. He tried to close his eyes, but he discovered he was unable to even blink.

Relief.

Finally, everything started slowing down.

The flashing light from the sun had peaked and was beginning to slow.

He could actually, with great effort, turn his head a little bit.

Slower.

Time was starting to settle back to its normal cadence.

Sterling was having a hard time maintaining consciousness as his brain was insisting on shutting down from the intense sensory input.

Slower.

When the Machine released its hold on Sterling, the rush of air to his nostrils was like food to a starving man. He didn't even notice the slight fall to the ground as he gulped in massive quantities of oxygen.

Lying prone on the ground was all he wanted to do at the moment and he savored just breathing for a while.

His head was still spinning from the travel and his limbs couldn't yet quite do his bidding, but he managed to lean his head to the side and vomit.

The warm breeze and the smell of the fields surrounding him tugged at Sterling's consciousness and he cheerfully let it go.

www.ingramcontent.com/pod-product-compliance
Lightning Source LLC
Chambersburg PA
CBHW032114280326
41933CB00009B/841